JOURNEY TO ENGLISH FLUENCY: 50 SHORT STORIES FOR B2 LEVEL LEARNERS

Elizabeth Snow

Fluent English Press

CONTENTS

1.

THE UNEXPECTED GUEST

Sophie had always enjoyed her quiet evenings at home. After a long day at work, she would curl up with a book, a cup of tea, and her cat, Muffin. Her life was predictable, and she liked it that way.

One rainy evening, as she was getting comfortable on her couch, there was a knock at the door. Sophie glanced at the clock. It was nearly 8 PM, and she wasn't expecting anyone. She hesitated for a moment, then got up to answer the door.

Standing on her doorstep was an elderly woman, drenched from the rain. Her clothes were soaked, and her hair was plastered to her face. She looked lost and tired.

"Hello?" Sophie said, unsure of what to do.

"Hello, dear," the woman replied, her voice shaky. "I'm sorry to bother you, but my car broke down a few blocks away, and my phone is dead. Can I come in and use your phone to call for help?"

Sophie was taken aback. She wasn't used to having strangers in her home, but she couldn't leave the woman out in the rain. "Of course, come in," she said, stepping aside.

The woman entered, leaving a small puddle of water on the floor. "Thank you so much," she said with a sigh of relief. "My name is Margaret."

"I'm Sophie," she replied, handing Margaret a towel. "Here, dry off a bit. I'll get you a cup of tea."

Margaret smiled gratefully. "You're very kind, Sophie."

As Sophie prepared the tea, Margaret dried herself and tried to call for help. But the phone call didn't go as planned. "I can't seem to reach anyone," Margaret said with a frown. "It looks like I'm stuck here for a while."

"That's alright," Sophie said. "You can stay here until you get through to someone. It's no trouble at all."

Margaret settled into a chair and accepted the cup of tea from Sophie. "You know, it's been a long time since I've had such a warm welcome from a stranger. It's nice to see that kindness still exists."

Sophie blushed. "It's nothing, really. I'm just glad I could help."

As they sipped their tea, they began to chat. Margaret shared stories of her younger days, and Sophie found herself fascinated by the tales of adventure and life lessons. Margaret had traveled the world, met interesting people, and experienced things Sophie could only dream of.

"You know, Sophie," Margaret said after a while, "life has a way of surprising us. We make plans, but sometimes, unexpected things happen. It's how we respond to those surprises that shape our lives."

Sophie nodded, feeling a sense of wisdom in Margaret's words. "I've always liked my routine, but maybe I've been too afraid of change."

"Change isn't always bad," Margaret replied. "Sometimes, it brings new opportunities and experiences that we never imagined. Like tonight. If my car hadn't broken down, I wouldn't have met you and had this lovely conversation."

Sophie smiled. "I guess you're right. It's easy to get stuck in a comfort zone and miss out on new experiences."

Margaret patted Sophie's hand. "Exactly. And you've shown me kindness tonight. Never underestimate the power of a small act of kindness. It can make a big difference in someone's life."

They continued talking for hours, sharing stories and laughter. Sophie felt a connection with Margaret that she hadn't felt with anyone in a long time. It was as if this unexpected visitor had brought a breath of fresh air into her life.

As the night grew late, Sophie realized how much she had enjoyed the evening. She had learned more in a few hours with Margaret than she had in years of living the same routine every day.

Finally, Margaret's phone rang. It was her son, who had been worried when she didn't come home. He was on his way to pick her up.

"Thank you again, Sophie," Margaret said as she stood to leave. "You've reminded me that there are still good people in the world. And you've taught me that it's never too late to make new friends."

Sophie walked Margaret to the door. "Thank you, Margaret. You've taught me that sometimes, the best things in life come from the unexpected."

As Margaret left, Sophie stood in the doorway, feeling a sense of fulfillment. She realized that her life didn't have to be a series of predictable events. Sometimes, embracing the unexpected could lead to the most meaningful experiences.

From that night on, Sophie decided to be more open to new experiences and to welcome the unexpected with open arms. And she never forgot the lessons she learned from the unexpected guest who had knocked on her door one rainy evening.

Drenched - Completely wet, usually because of being in water or rain.

- Sophie was drenched after being caught in the sudden downpour without an umbrella.

Taken aback - To be surprised or shocked by something unexpected.

- Margaret was taken aback when Sophie invited her into her home without hesitation.

Sigh of relief - A feeling of comfort or calmness after a worry or danger has passed.

- Margaret let out a sigh of relief when Sophie offered her a place to stay until help arrived.

Fascinated - Extremely interested in something or someone.

- Sophie was fascinated by Margaret's stories of travel and adventure.

Embracing - To accept willingly or eagerly; to hold someone or something close.

- Sophie decided to embrace the unexpected visitor and invite her in from the rain.

Fulfillment - Satisfaction or happiness as a result of fully developing one's abilities or character.

- Sophie felt a sense of fulfillment after helping Margaret and learning from her.

2.

LOST IN THE CITY

Emma had always dreamed of visiting Paris. She had saved up for years and finally booked a two-week vacation in the beautiful city. Her excitement knew no bounds as she stepped off the plane and into the bustling Parisian airport. She had her guidebook, a list of must-see places, and a basic understanding of French. She was ready for an adventure.

After settling into her cozy hotel room, Emma set out to explore the city. She marveled at the Eiffel Tower, wandered through the Louvre, and enjoyed a croissant at a charming café. Everything was perfect, just as she had imagined.

One evening, after a delightful dinner in a small bistro, Emma decided to take a walk. The sun was setting, casting a golden glow over the city. She walked along the Seine, taking in the sights and sounds of Paris at dusk. Lost in her thoughts, she didn't notice how far she had wandered from her hotel.

As the sky grew darker, Emma realized she had no idea where she was. She pulled out her map, but the street names looked different in the dim light. Her phone's battery was low, and she couldn't use it to find her way back. Panic began to set in.

"Excusez-moi," she said, approaching a passerby. "Pouvez-vous m'aider? Je suis perdue."

The man looked at her apologetically. "Je suis désolé, je ne parle pas anglais," he said, shaking his head.

Emma tried asking a few more people, but each time, she was met with the same response. She felt tears of frustration welling up in her eyes. How could she have been so careless?

Just as she was about to give up, she heard a voice behind her. "Excuse me, do you need help?" Turning around, she saw a young woman with a friendly smile. "I heard you speaking English. Are you lost?"

Emma nodded, relieved to hear her native language. "Yes, I am. I can't find my way back to my hotel, and my phone is almost dead."

The woman extended her hand. "I'm Claire. I live here in Paris. I can help you find your way."

Emma shook her hand gratefully. "Thank you so much, Claire. I'm Emma. I don't know what I would have done without your help."

"Let's start by figuring out where your hotel is," Claire said, pulling out her phone. "Do you remember the name or the address?"

Emma racked her brain. "It's called Hôtel de la Paix, and it's near a metro station, but I can't remember which one."

Claire nodded and quickly looked up the hotel. "Got it. It's near the Saint-Michel station. We're not too far from there. Come on, I'll walk you back."

As they walked, Emma felt her anxiety fade away. Claire was easy to talk to, and they chatted about their lives. Claire told Emma about her job as a graphic designer and her love for the city. Emma shared stories about her hometown and her adventures in Paris so far.

"You know," Claire said, "getting lost in a foreign city isn't always a bad thing. It can lead to the most unexpected experiences and encounters."

Emma smiled. "You're right. I was so scared at first, but now I'm grateful. I got to meet you and see a different side of Paris."

They continued walking, and soon they reached the Saint-Michel metro station. From there, it was only a short distance to Emma's hotel. As they stood outside the hotel, Emma turned to Claire.

"I can't thank you enough, Claire. You saved my evening."

Claire waved it off. "It was my pleasure. I'm glad I could help. And who knows, maybe we'll run into each other again during your stay."

Emma nodded. "I hope so. You've made my trip even more memorable."

They exchanged contact information, and Claire gave Emma some tips on places to visit and things to do in the city. With a final hug, they parted ways, and Emma entered her hotel, feeling a mix of relief and gratitude.

That night, as Emma lay in bed, she reflected on the day's events. Getting lost in the city had been frightening, but it had also brought her an unexpected friend. She realized that sometimes, the best experiences come from the most unexpected moments. It was a lesson she would carry with her for the rest of her travels.

Over the next few days, Emma and Claire met up a few times, exploring the city together. Claire showed Emma hidden gems that weren't in the guidebooks, and Emma shared her enthusiasm and fresh perspective with Claire. They laughed, took photos, and made memories that would last a lifetime.

When it was time for Emma to leave Paris, she felt a pang of sadness. But she knew she would always have a friend in the city of lights. As she boarded the plane back home, she looked out at the skyline one last time, grateful for the unexpected adventure that had made her trip so special.

Emma's experience taught her that even when things don't go

as planned, there's always something positive to be found. It reminded her to stay open to new experiences and to embrace the unknown with an open heart. And most importantly, it showed her the incredible kindness of strangers, a lesson she would never forget.

Bustling - Full of energetic and noisy activity.

- Emma arrived at the bustling Parisian airport, excited to begin her adventure in the city.

Marveled - To be filled with wonder or astonishment.

- Emma marveled at the beauty of the Eiffel Tower as she stood beneath its towering structure.

Wandered - To move about or travel aimlessly or without any destination in mind.

- After visiting the Louvre, Emma wandered through the nearby streets, soaking in the atmosphere of Paris.

Panic - Sudden strong fear that prevents reasonable thought or action.

- Emma felt panic creeping in as she realized she was lost in an unfamiliar part of the city.

Relieved - Feeling happy because something unpleasant has stopped or has not happened.

- Emma was relieved when Claire offered to help her find her way back to the hotel.

Gratefully - Feeling or showing thanks because of something done or given.

- Emma shook Claire's hand gratefully, thankful for her assistance in navigating the streets of Paris.

Anxiety - A feeling of worry, nervousness, or unease about something with an uncertain outcome.

- Emma's anxiety faded away as Claire guided her closer to her hotel, reassuring her along the way.

Memorable - Worth remembering or easily remembered, especially because of being special or unusual.

- Meeting Claire and exploring hidden Parisian gems made Emma's trip truly memorable.

Enthusiasm - A strong feeling of excitement and interest.

- Emma shared her enthusiasm for French cuisine as she and Claire enjoyed a meal together at a local bistro.

3.

THE SECRET GARDEN

Anna and Ben were siblings who loved to explore. They lived in a quiet village surrounded by hills and forests. One summer day, while their parents were busy, they decided to go on an adventure. Their curiosity often led them to new places, but today, they would find something truly magical.

"Let's go to the old mansion," Anna suggested. The mansion was at the edge of the village and had been abandoned for years. People said it was haunted, but Anna and Ben didn't believe in ghosts.

"Sure," Ben agreed. "Maybe we'll find something interesting."

They packed some snacks and set off on their bikes. The path to the mansion was overgrown with weeds, and the building itself looked spooky, but Anna and Ben were determined. They parked their bikes and approached the gate, which was locked.

"How do we get in?" Ben asked.

Anna spotted a gap in the hedge. "We can squeeze through here," she said. Carefully, they wriggled through the bushes and found themselves in the mansion's garden.

The garden was a mess, with tall grass and wild plants everywhere. But amidst the chaos, Anna noticed something unusual. "Look, Ben! There's a path," she pointed out.

Indeed, there was a narrow path, almost hidden by the overgrown plants. They followed it, pushing through the underbrush, until they came to a large stone wall covered in ivy.

"What's behind this wall?" Ben wondered aloud.

"Only one way to find out," Anna replied, feeling around the ivy. Her fingers brushed against something metallic. "A door handle!" she exclaimed. She pulled the ivy aside, revealing an old wooden door.

With some effort, they managed to push the door open. What they saw on the other side took their breath away. The garden inside was beautiful, filled with flowers of every color, neatly trimmed bushes, and a sparkling fountain in the center.

"This is amazing," Ben said in awe. "It's like a secret paradise."

Anna nodded, equally amazed. "Who do you think takes care of it?"

They wandered around the garden, admiring the flowers and listening to the sound of the fountain. In one corner, they found a small bench and sat down to rest.

"This place feels magical," Anna said. "I wonder why it's hidden."

Just then, they heard a soft voice behind them. "It's hidden because it's special."

Startled, they turned around to see an elderly woman standing there. She had kind eyes and a gentle smile.

"I'm sorry if we intruded," Ben said quickly. "We were just exploring."

The woman chuckled. "No need to apologize. I'm glad you found the garden. It's been a long time since anyone came here."

"Do you take care of this place?" Anna asked.

The woman nodded. "Yes, I do. My name is Mrs. Willow. This garden has been in my family for generations. It has always been a place of peace and beauty."

"It's incredible," Anna said. "Why is it kept a secret?"

Mrs. Willow sat down on the bench and motioned for them to join her. "This garden is a sanctuary," she explained. "A place where people can come to find peace and reflect. It's hidden to protect its tranquility."

Anna and Ben listened intently. They felt honored to have discovered such a special place.

"Can we help you take care of it?" Ben asked. "We would love to come here and help."

Mrs. Willow smiled warmly. "I would love that. It's a big job for one person, and I'm not as young as I used to be."

From that day on, Anna and Ben visited the secret garden regularly. They helped Mrs. Willow with planting, watering, and trimming the plants. They learned about different types of flowers and how to care for them. The garden became their favorite place, a sanctuary where they could escape the hustle and bustle of daily life.

As they worked, Mrs. Willow shared stories about the garden's history. She told them about her ancestors who had planted the first flowers and built the fountain. She explained how the garden had been a place of healing and inspiration for many people over the years.

One day, while they were planting new flowers, Anna asked, "Mrs. Willow, do you ever feel lonely here?"

Mrs. Willow paused and looked at the vibrant blooms around her. "Sometimes," she admitted. "But the garden gives me comfort. And now that I have you two, I feel less lonely."

Anna and Ben exchanged smiles. They were happy to be part of something so special. They realized that the garden was not just a place of beauty, but also a place of connection and friendship.

As the summer days passed, the garden flourished under their care. The flowers bloomed brightly, and the fountain sparkled in the sunlight. Anna and Ben felt a deep sense of satisfaction and joy in their work.

One evening, as they were getting ready to leave, Mrs. Willow handed them each a small key. "These are for you," she said. "The keys to the garden. You are its guardians now."

Anna and Ben were speechless. They felt a surge of pride and gratitude. "Thank you, Mrs. Willow," Ben said. "We'll take good care of it."

Mrs. Willow nodded, her eyes twinkling with warmth. "I know you will."

From that moment on, Anna and Ben made it their

mission to protect and nurture the secret garden. They visited it even after the summer ended, tending to the plants and ensuring the garden remained a place of beauty and peace.

Their friends often wondered where Anna and Ben spent so much of their time, but they never revealed the garden's location. It was their special place, a hidden gem that connected them not only to nature but also to Mrs. Willow and the generations before them.

As the years went by, the bond between Anna, Ben, and Mrs. Willow grew stronger. They celebrated birthdays and special occasions in the garden, filling it with laughter and joy. Mrs. Willow shared more stories and wisdom, and Anna and Ben cherished every moment.

One sunny afternoon, Anna and Ben arrived at the garden to find Mrs. Willow waiting for them with a picnic basket. "I thought we could have a picnic today," she said, her smile brighter than ever.

They spent the day enjoying the delicious food and each other's company. As they sat under the shade of a large tree, Mrs. Willow took Anna and Ben's hands in hers. "You've brought so much life and love to this garden," she said softly. "And to me."

Anna squeezed her hand. "You've done the same for us, Mrs. Willow. This garden is a part of us now."

Mrs. Willow nodded, her eyes glistening with tears of happiness. "Promise me you'll always take care of it, and each other."

"We promise," Ben said, his voice filled with emotion.

Years later, when Anna and Ben were adults with children of their own, they continued to visit the secret garden. They taught their children about the flowers, the fountain, and the importance of caring for such a special place. The garden thrived, a living testament to the love and dedication of those who tended to it.

Mrs. Willow had passed on, but her spirit remained in every bloom and every breeze that rustled the leaves. Anna and Ben felt her presence, guiding them and reminding them of the lessons they had learned.

The secret garden became a sanctuary for many more generations, each one finding peace and inspiration within its walls. Anna and Ben's children and grandchildren grew up with the stories of Mrs. Willow and the hidden paradise she had shared with them.

The garden, once a hidden gem discovered by two curious siblings, became a legacy of love, friendship, and the beauty of nature. It stood as a reminder that even the smallest places can hold the greatest treasures and that the connections we make with others can transform our lives in the most unexpected ways.

Abandoned - Left empty or unoccupied; deserted.

- The mansion at the edge of the village had been abandoned for many years, rumored to be haunted.

Spooky - Eerie or frightening in a way that suggests the presence of ghosts or supernatural beings.

- Anna and Ben found the old mansion spooky, but they were eager to explore its mysteries.

Intruded - To enter a place or situation where you are not welcome or invited.

- Ben apologized to Mrs. Willow, worried they had intruded upon her peaceful garden.

Sanctuary - A place of refuge or safety.

- Mrs. Willow described the secret garden as a sanctuary where people could find peace and tranquility.

Tranquility - The quality or state of being calm and peaceful.

- Anna and Ben loved the garden for its tranquility, away from the noise and busyness of their village.

Guardians - People who protect or defend something.

- Mrs. Willow entrusted Anna and Ben with the keys to the garden, making them its guardians.

Cherished - To value or care for something deeply.

- Anna and Ben cherished their time spent with Mrs. Willow in the garden, learning about its history and beauty.

Legacy - Something handed down from one generation to the next; a lasting impact or contribution.

- The secret garden became a legacy of love and friendship, passed down through generations of caretakers.

Inspiration - The process of being mentally stimulated to do or feel something creative or worthwhile.

- Mrs. Willow found inspiration in the garden's beauty and in the company of Anna and Ben.

Transform - To change in form, appearance, or character.

- The secret garden transformed from a neglected space into a vibrant sanctuary under Anna and Ben's care.

4.

THE GREAT ESCAPE

Max the hamster had always been curious. He lived in a cozy cage in Emma's room, filled with tunnels, a wheel, and lots of soft bedding. Emma loved Max and took good care of him, making sure he had everything he needed. But Max wanted to see more of the world beyond his cage.

One evening, Emma forgot to close the cage door properly. Max noticed this immediately. His tiny heart raced with excitement. This was his chance to explore! He cautiously stepped out of the cage and onto Emma's desk. The house was quiet; Emma and her family were downstairs watching TV.

Max climbed down the desk leg and onto the floor. The world seemed so much bigger outside his cage. He darted across the room, heading for the open door. Once in the hallway, Max paused to sniff the air. He could smell food, hear distant sounds, and see shadows moving. Everything was new and exciting.

The first stop on his adventure was the kitchen. He followed the smell of food and found a small piece of cheese on the floor. Max nibbled on it happily. "This is so much better than my regular food," he thought.

After his snack, Max continued exploring. He saw the big front door slightly open. The cool night air was inviting. With a burst of courage, Max squeezed through the gap and found himself outside. The grass felt strange under his tiny feet, and the night sky was vast above him. He saw stars twinkling and felt a gentle breeze.

Max wandered through the garden, marveling at the plants and flowers. Suddenly, he heard a rustling sound. He froze, his whiskers twitching. Out from behind a bush came a large cat. Max's heart pounded. He knew cats were dangerous for small creatures like him.

The cat, named Whiskers, spotted Max and crouched low, ready to pounce. Max ran as fast as his little legs could carry him, darting under bushes and between flower pots. He found a small hole in the fence and squeezed through just in time. Whiskers stopped at the fence, frustrated, and finally walked away.

Max found himself in the neighbor's yard. He was tired but safe for now. He climbed onto a rock to rest. As he looked around, he saw other animals—a squirrel chattering in a tree and birds settling in for the night. "What an adventure," he thought, feeling a mix of excitement and exhaustion.

As the night went on, Max explored more of the neighborhood. He found a small playground with swings and slides. He climbed up the slide, feeling proud of his bravery. From the top, he could see the whole playground. He wished Emma could see him now.

Meanwhile, Emma had gone to check on Max and found his cage empty. She panicked, searching the house frantically. "Mom, Dad, Max is gone!" she cried. Her parents helped her look, but there was no sign of Max.

Emma decided to search outside. She grabbed a flashlight and called for Max softly. "Max, where are you? Come back, please," she pleaded. Her heart ached with worry. Max was small and vulnerable; she hoped he was safe.

Max, hearing Emma's voice in the distance, felt a strong urge to find her. He missed his cozy cage and the safety it provided. Following the sound of her voice, he made his way back through the gardens and yards. He was determined to find his way home.

Emma's flashlight beam caught a tiny movement near the fence. She rushed over and saw Max peeking through a hole. "Max! There you are," she cried with relief, gently picking him up. Max snuggled into her hand, feeling safe again.

Back in her room, Emma checked Max for any injuries. He seemed tired but unharmed. She placed him back in his cage, making sure the door was securely closed this time. "You had quite an adventure, didn't you?" she said, smiling at him.

Max ran to his water bottle for a long drink, then burrowed into his bedding. He was happy to be home. The outside world was exciting, but it was also scary. His cage, with its familiar smells and safety, felt just right.

As Emma got ready for bed, she thought about Max's great escape. She realized how much she cared for her little friend and how important it was to keep him safe. She made a mental note to always double-check his cage door.

The next day, Emma told her friends at school about Max's adventure. They were amazed at how brave he had been. "Your hamster is like a little superhero," one friend said.

Emma laughed. "He is, isn't he? But I'm just glad he's back home."

That night, as Max ran on his wheel, he thought about his adventure. It had been thrilling, but he was content to be back in his cozy home with Emma. He knew he was loved and cared for, and that was the best feeling in the world.

Curious - Eager to know or learn something.

o   Max the hamster had always been curious about the world beyond his cage.

Darted - Moved suddenly and quickly.

- o   Max darted across the room, excited to explore the open door.

Nibbled - Took small bites of something.

- o   Max nibbled on the cheese he found in the kitchen, enjoying its taste.

Vast - Very large in size, extent, or quantity.

- o   Max looked up at the vast night sky, amazed by the stars twinkling above him.

Pounced - To spring or swoop suddenly and take aggressive action.

- o   Whiskers the cat pounced when she spotted Max in the garden.

Frustrated - Feeling or expressing distress and annoyance, especially because of inability to change or achieve something.

- o   Whiskers was frustrated when Max escaped through the hole in the fence.

Playground - An outdoor area provided for children to play in, especially at a school or public park.

- o   Max found a small playground with swings and slides during his adventure.

Frantically - In a hurried, disorganized, and chaotic manner.

- o   Emma searched frantically for Max when she realized he had escaped from his cage.

Panicked - To feel or cause to feel sudden uncontrollable fear or anxiety.

- o   Emma panicked when she couldn't find Max in his cage.

Burrowed - To move under or as if under something, especially in search of refuge or shelter.

- o   Max burrowed into his bedding, feeling safe and secure back in his cage.

5.

THE LAST LEAF

Anna and Jane were best friends, living in a small apartment building in the city. They had known each other for years, sharing countless memories and always supporting each other. One autumn, Anna became very ill. She stayed in bed most days, feeling weak and tired.

Jane was worried about her friend. She visited Anna every day, bringing food and reading to her. Anna's room had a large window that overlooked a small courtyard with a single tree. As autumn progressed, the leaves on the tree began to fall.

One day, as Jane was reading to Anna, they both noticed the tree outside. Its branches were almost bare, with only a few leaves hanging on. "Look at that tree, Jane," Anna said weakly. "I feel like that tree. I'm losing hope, just like it's losing its leaves."

Jane squeezed Anna's hand. "Don't talk like that, Anna. You'll get better. You just need to stay strong."

Anna shook her head. "I don't think I can, Jane. When the last leaf falls, I think I will too."

Jane felt a lump in her throat but tried to stay positive. "That's just a silly idea, Anna. You're much stronger than a leaf on a tree."

Days went by, and Anna's condition did not improve. Jane noticed that Anna spent a lot of time staring out the window, watching the last few leaves cling to the tree. Each day, more leaves fell, and Anna grew weaker.

One evening, Jane had an idea. She spoke to Mr. Behrman, an elderly artist who lived in the building. Mr. Behrman was known for his grumpy demeanor, but Jane knew he had a kind heart. She explained Anna's situation and her fear about the last leaf falling.

Mr. Behrman listened carefully. "So, you want me to paint a leaf on the wall outside her window?" he asked, raising an eyebrow.

"Yes," Jane replied. "I know it sounds strange, but I think it might give her hope."

Mr. Behrman thought for a moment and then nodded. "I'll do it tonight, after it gets dark. She won't see me working."

That night, a strong wind blew through the city, rattling windows and shaking trees. Jane was worried that the last leaf might fall, but she trusted Mr. Behrman. Early the next morning, she visited Anna. She found her friend gazing out the window with a look of amazement.

"Jane, look! The last leaf didn't fall. It's still there!" Anna exclaimed, her eyes bright with hope.

Jane smiled, hiding her own surprise. "See, Anna? I told you that you are stronger than a leaf."

As the days passed, Anna's spirits lifted. She began to eat more, gained some strength, and even sat up in bed to read. She continued to watch the last leaf, feeling inspired by its resilience.

Jane was overjoyed to see Anna improving. She visited Mr. Behrman to thank him. "You saved my friend," she said, tears in her eyes. "I can't thank you enough."

Mr. Behrman waved his hand dismissively. "It was nothing. Just a little paint and some late-night work." But Jane could see the pride in his eyes.

One day, Anna asked Jane about Mr. Behrman. "He painted that leaf, didn't he?" she asked softly.

Jane nodded. "Yes, he did. He wanted to give you hope."

Anna smiled, tears in her eyes. "He did more than that. He gave me a reason to fight."

Winter came, and Anna continued to get better. She was soon able to leave her bed and walk around the apartment. One day, she visited Mr. Behrman to thank him personally.

"Mr. Behrman, you saved my life," Anna said, hugging him tightly.

Mr. Behrman patted her back awkwardly, his eyes moist. "I'm glad you're better, Anna. That's all that matters."

As spring approached, Anna and Jane watched the tree outside Anna's window. New buds began to appear, and soon the tree was full of fresh green leaves. Anna felt like she was coming back to life along with the tree.

One evening, Anna and Jane invited Mr. Behrman for dinner. They wanted to celebrate Anna's recovery and thank him properly. During the meal, Anna raised her glass.

"To friendship, hope, and the last leaf," she toasted.

"To the last leaf," Jane and Mr. Behrman echoed, smiling.

Anna looked at her friends with gratitude. "I learned something important during my illness. Sometimes, hope comes from the most unexpected places. We just have to keep believing."

Jane nodded. "And sometimes, it takes a little help from friends and a bit of creativity to keep that hope alive."

The three friends shared a warm, joyful evening, feeling grateful for the simple yet powerful things that can change lives. Anna knew she would never forget the last leaf and the lessons it had taught her about hope, strength, and the enduring power of friendship.

Courtyard - An open space surrounded by walls or buildings, typically within a building complex.

- Anna's room had a large window that overlooked a small courtyard with a single tree.

Lump - A small, compact mass of substance.

- Jane felt a lump in her throat but tried to stay positive for Anna.

Demeanor - Outward behavior or bearing.

- Mr. Behrman was known for his grumpy demeanor, but Jane knew he had a kind heart.

Resilience - The capacity to recover quickly from difficulties; toughness.

- Anna felt inspired by the resilience of the last leaf clinging to the tree outside her window.

Amazement - A feeling of great surprise or wonder.

- "Jane, look! The last leaf didn't fall. It's still there!" Anna exclaimed in amazement.

Dismissively - In a manner that suggests that something or someone is unworthy of consideration.

- Mr. Behrman waved his hand dismissively, downplaying his role in painting the leaf.

Buds - A compact knoblike growth on a plant that develops into a leaf, flower, or shoot.

- As spring approached, new buds began to appear on the tree outside Anna's window.

Awkwardly - In a clumsy or uncomfortable way.

- Mr. Behrman patted Anna's back awkwardly, touched by her gratitude.

Gratitude - The quality of being thankful; readiness to show appreciation for and to return kindness.

- Anna looked at her friends with gratitude during their dinner together.

Enduring - Continuing or long-lasting.

- Anna learned about the enduring power of friendship from her experience with the last leaf.

6.

THE MYSTERIOUS LETTER

Mark was an ordinary young man. He lived in a small town and worked at a local bookstore. His life was simple and routine. Every day, he walked to work, helped customers, and enjoyed reading in his free time. But one day, something unexpected happened.

It was a rainy Tuesday morning when Mark received a letter. This was unusual because he rarely got mail. The envelope was old and yellowed, with no return address. Curious, Mark opened it carefully. Inside was a single piece of paper with neat, handwritten words:

"Dear Mark, I know you don't know me, but I need your help. Please meet me at the old clock tower at midnight tonight.

A Friend"

Mark was puzzled. Who could have sent this letter? He didn't recognize the handwriting, and he couldn't think of anyone who would write such a mysterious note. He showed the letter to his friend, Lucy, who worked with him at the bookstore.

"Wow, Mark, this is really strange," Lucy said, examining the letter. "Are you going to go?"

Mark hesitated. "I'm not sure. It could be a prank, or it could be dangerous. But... I'm also curious. What if someone really needs my help?"

Lucy nodded thoughtfully. "Maybe you should go, but be careful. Take your phone and let me know what happens."

That night, Mark couldn't stop thinking about the letter. The words played over and over in his mind. By the time midnight approached, he had decided to go. He put on his raincoat, grabbed his phone, and headed to the old clock tower.

The clock tower was a tall, abandoned building on the edge of town. It was a place kids often told ghost stories about. Mark felt a chill as he approached, but he pushed his fear aside and walked inside. The tower was dark and silent, except for the sound of rain outside.

"Hello?" Mark called out, his voice echoing through the empty space. "Is anyone here?"

There was no answer. He walked further in, his footsteps echoing. Suddenly, he heard a noise behind him. He turned quickly and saw a shadowy figure standing in the doorway.

"Who are you?" Mark asked, trying to sound brave.

The figure stepped forward into the light. It was an old man with kind eyes and a gentle smile. "Mark, thank you for coming," the man said. "I know this must seem strange, but I needed to speak with you."

"Who are you?" Mark repeated.

"My name is Mr. Thompson," the man replied. "I used to live in this town many years ago. I knew your grandparents very well. They were good friends of mine."

Mark was surprised. "You knew my grandparents? But why did you ask me to come here?"

Mr. Thompson sighed. "I have something very important to tell you. Your grandparents left something for you, something very special. But they wanted you to find it on your own, when you were ready."

Mark's curiosity grew. "What did they leave for me?"

The old man reached into his coat and pulled out a small, wooden box. "This box contains a key," he explained. "The key opens a door in the old house where your grandparents lived. Inside, you will find their most treasured possession. They wanted you to have it."

Mark took the box, feeling a mix of excitement and nervousness. "Why did they want me to find it this way?"

"Your grandparents believed in the importance of discovery and adventure," Mr. Thompson said with a smile. "They wanted you to experience the thrill of finding something valuable on your own."

Mark thanked Mr. Thompson and promised to visit his grandparents' old house the next day. He left the clock tower, his mind racing with questions. What could be inside the house? Why was it so important?

The next morning, Mark woke up early and made his way to the old house. It had been empty for years, but he still had the key to the front door. He entered the house, feeling a wave of nostalgia. He remembered visiting his grandparents here when he was a child.

He went to the attic, where he found a small door hidden behind some old boxes. He used the key from the wooden box to unlock it. Inside, he found a beautiful, antique chest. He opened the chest and found it filled with letters, photos, and a diary.

As Mark read through the letters and diary, he discovered stories about his grandparents' lives, their adventures, and their love for each other. He found old photographs of them traveling the world, helping people, and living life to the fullest. It was a treasure trove of memories and life lessons.

Tears filled Mark's eyes as he read about their hopes and dreams. He felt a deep connection to them and a renewed sense of purpose. He realized that his grandparents wanted him to learn about their lives so he could find inspiration and guidance.

Mark returned to the bookstore with the chest, eager to share his discovery with Lucy. "You won't believe what I found," he told her, his voice full of excitement.

Lucy listened intently as Mark told her everything. "Wow, Mark, that's amazing," she said. "Your grandparents sound like incredible people."

"They were," Mark replied, smiling. "And now I feel like I know them better than ever. I'm so grateful for this experience. It has changed my life."

From that day on, Mark felt a new sense of direction. He was inspired by his grandparents' stories to live his life with more adventure and purpose. He continued to work at the bookstore, but he also started writing about his own experiences, hoping to inspire others just as his grandparents had inspired him.

Routine - a sequence of actions regularly followed; a fixed program.

- Mark's life was simple and routine, with daily walks to work and evenings spent reading.

Envelop - to completely enclose or surround something.

- The old letter was enveloped in a yellowed envelope with no return address.

Puzzled - unable to understand; perplexed.

- Mark was puzzled by the mysterious letter and its

unknown sender.

Hesitate - to pause before saying or doing something, especially through uncertainty.

- Mark hesitated before deciding whether to go to the old clock tower as instructed in the letter.

Abandoned - deserted or left behind.

- The old clock tower was an abandoned building on the edge of town.

Echo - a sound or series of sounds caused by the reflection of sound waves from a surface back to the listener.

- Mark's voice echoed through the dark and silent tower as he called out.

Treasured - held dear; cherished.

- Inside the antique chest, Mark found his grandparents' treasured letters, photos, and diary.

Nostalgia - a sentimental longing or affection for the past.

- Mark felt a wave of nostalgia as he entered his grandparents' old house and explored the attic.

Discovery - the act or process of finding or learning something for the first time.

- Mark's discovery of the chest in the attic revealed his grandparents' hidden treasures.

Adventure - an unusual and exciting or daring experience.

- Mark's journey to uncover his grandparents' legacy was an adventure that changed his life.

Inspiration - the process of being mentally stimulated to do or feel something, especially to do something creative.

- Mark found inspiration in his grandparents' stories to live his life with more purpose and adventure.

Transformative - causing a marked change in someone or something.

- Mark's encounter with the mysterious letter was transformative, leading him to discover a deeper connection with his family history.

Legacy - something handed down from a predecessor or from the past.

- Mark uncovered his grandparents' legacy through the letters and diary found in the chest.

Purpose - the reason for which something is done or created; the reason for which something exists.

- Mark felt a renewed sense of purpose after learning about his grandparents' lives and experiences.

Direction - a course along which someone or something moves or is aimed to move.

- Mark gained a new sense of direction in life, inspired by his grandparents' adventurous spirits.

7.

THE LIGHTHOUSE KEEPER

Ethan had been the lighthouse keeper for nearly thirty years. He lived in a small, cozy house at the base of the lighthouse, which stood tall and proud on a rocky cliff overlooking the sea. His job was simple yet important: keep the light burning to guide ships safely through the treacherous waters.

Every day, Ethan would climb the winding stairs to the top of the lighthouse. He would clean the lenses, check the oil, and make sure everything was in perfect working order. At night, he would light the lamp and watch as the bright beam cut through the darkness, casting a reassuring glow over the ocean.

One stormy evening, as Ethan was preparing for another long night, he noticed something unusual. The waves were crashing violently against the rocks, and the wind was howling like a wild beast. As he looked out to sea, he saw a faint light flickering in the distance. It was a distress signal from a ship in trouble.

Ethan grabbed his binoculars and focused on the light. Through the rain and fog, he could make out the silhouette of a large ship, being tossed around by the angry waves. He knew he had to act quickly. The ship was in serious danger, and he was their only hope.

He ran to his radio and contacted the coast guard. "This is Ethan, the lighthouse keeper. There's a ship in distress near the lighthouse. They need immediate assistance."

"Roger that, Ethan," the coast guard replied. "We'll send a rescue team right away. Keep your light steady and guide them as best as you can."

Ethan felt a surge of determination. He rushed back to the top of the lighthouse and made sure the light was shining as brightly as possible. He then took out his signal lamp and started sending Morse code messages to the ship, hoping the crew would see and understand.

"Stay calm. Help is on the way. Follow the light," he signaled.

The ship responded with a brief flash of light, indicating that they had received his message. Ethan continued to send reassuring signals, guiding the ship toward the lighthouse. He knew the waters around the cliff were dangerous, full of hidden rocks and strong currents. One wrong move could be disastrous.

As the minutes ticked by, the storm seemed to intensify. The wind howled louder, and the rain lashed against the windows of the lighthouse. Ethan's heart pounded in his chest as he watched the ship struggle to stay afloat. He could see the crew working frantically on the deck, trying to keep the vessel steady.

Finally, after what felt like an eternity, Ethan saw the lights of the coast guard's rescue boats approaching. They moved swiftly through the rough waters, expertly navigating the waves. Ethan continued to signal the ship, guiding them toward the rescue boats.

The rescue team reached the ship just in time. They threw ropes and life preservers to the crew, helping them to safety. Ethan watched with a mix of relief and anxiety as each member of the crew was pulled aboard the rescue boats. He kept his light steady, ensuring the rescuers could see their way back to shore.

Once the last crew member was safe, the coast guard radioed Ethan. "The ship's crew is safe, Ethan. Thanks to your guidance, we were able to rescue them all."

Ethan let out a long sigh of relief. "Thank you for your swift response," he replied. "I'm just glad they're safe."

The storm eventually passed, leaving a calm sea and a clear sky in its wake. The next morning, as the sun rose over the horizon, Ethan climbed to the top of the lighthouse once more. He looked out at the sea, now peaceful and serene, and thought about the events of the previous night.

Later that day, Ethan received a visit from the captain of the ship and his crew. They had come to thank him personally for his bravery and quick thinking.

"Thank you, Ethan," the captain said, shaking his hand firmly. "You saved our lives. Without your help, we wouldn't be here today."

Ethan smiled modestly. "I was just doing my job," he said. "I'm glad I could help."

The crew presented Ethan with a plaque, engraved with their gratitude. It read: "To Ethan, the lighthouse keeper, for your unwavering dedication and heroic actions. Thank you for guiding us to safety."

Ethan felt a deep sense of pride and fulfillment as he accepted the plaque. He realized that his role as the lighthouse keeper was more than just a job. It was a responsibility and a calling. He was there to protect and guide those in need, to be a beacon of hope in the darkest of times.

From that day on, Ethan continued his duties with renewed purpose. He knew that every time he lit the lamp, he was not just guiding ships; he was safeguarding lives. And that made all the difference.

Cozy

- o Definition: Warm, comfortable, and pleasant, especially in a small space.
- o Sample: Ethan lived in a small, cozy house at the base of the lighthouse, enjoying the sound of the waves crashing against the rocks.

Treacherous

- o Definition: Very dangerous and difficult to deal with.
- o Sample: Ethan's job as a lighthouse keeper involved guiding ships through treacherous waters with his steady beacon of light.

Distress

- o Definition: Extreme anxiety, sorrow, or pain; suffering.
- o Sample: Ethan noticed a distress signal from a ship caught in a storm, prompting him to take immediate action to assist them.

Reassuring

- o Definition: Serving to restore confidence and remove doubts; comforting.
- o Sample: Ethan's lighthouse beam cast a reassuring glow over the stormy sea, guiding ships safely through the night.

Determination

- o Definition: Firmness of purpose; resoluteness.
- o Sample: Ethan felt a surge of determination as he worked tirelessly to guide the ship to safety through the storm.

Frantically

- o Definition: In a hurried, excited, or disorganized manner.
- o Sample: The crew of the distressed ship worked frantically to secure their vessel as Ethan signaled them with Morse code from the lighthouse.

Swiftly

- o Definition: At high speed; quickly.
- o Sample: The coast guard's rescue boats moved swiftly through the rough waters to reach the ship Ethan was guiding towards safety.

Modestly

- o Definition: In an unassuming or moderate manner; without boasting.
- o Sample: Ethan smiled modestly when the ship's captain thanked him for his bravery and quick thinking during the storm.

Fulfillment

- o Definition: Satisfaction or happiness as a result of fully developing one's abilities or character.
- o Sample: Ethan felt deep fulfillment knowing that his role as a lighthouse keeper had a direct impact on saving lives during emergencies at sea.

8.

THE ART OF FORGIVENESS

Lucy and Emma had been friends since childhood. They did everything together, from attending the same school to playing in the same soccer team. They were inseparable. But as they grew older, their paths began to diverge. Lucy loved painting and spent most of her time in art class, while Emma was passionate about writing and joined the school newspaper.

One day, Emma wrote an article for the school newspaper about the upcoming art exhibition, where Lucy was going to display her paintings. Emma was proud of her friend and wanted to showcase her talent. But in her excitement, she mistakenly wrote that Lucy's art was "simple and unoriginal," instead of the "beautiful and unique" she had meant to say. It was an unfortunate typo, but the damage was done.

Lucy was heartbroken when she read the article. She felt betrayed by her best friend. "How could Emma say such things about my art?" she thought. She felt a mix of anger and sadness, and decided to confront Emma about it.

After school, Lucy found Emma in the library, working on another article. "Emma, can we talk?" she asked, trying to keep her voice steady.

Emma looked up, surprised to see the upset look on Lucy's face. "Sure, what's wrong?"

Lucy handed Emma the newspaper, pointing to the article. "How could you write this about me? You know how much my art means to me!"

Emma's eyes widened as she read the mistake. "Oh no, Lucy, I'm so sorry! It was a typo! I didn't mean to write that at all. I meant to say your art is beautiful and unique."

Lucy's anger was still boiling. "A typo? Do you know how many people have read this? Everyone thinks you don't believe in me or my art!"

Emma felt terrible. "I promise I'll fix it. I'll write a correction in the next issue. Please, Lucy, believe me. I never meant to hurt you."

But Lucy was too hurt to listen. She stormed out of the library, leaving Emma feeling helpless and guilty.

Days passed, and the tension between them grew. They avoided each other at school, and their friends noticed the change. Both Lucy and Emma felt the pain of the broken friendship, but neither knew how to bridge the gap.

One afternoon, while sitting alone in her room, Lucy received a message from Emma. It was an invitation to the park where they used to play as children. Lucy hesitated, but curiosity got the better of her, and she decided to go.

When Lucy arrived at the park, she found Emma sitting on their favorite bench, holding a sketchbook. "Lucy, I know I hurt you, and I'm truly sorry. I brought you something."

Emma handed Lucy the sketchbook. Inside were drawings Emma had made of all their favorite memories together—playing soccer, attending art class, even moments from their school trips. Each drawing had a caption, expressing Emma's gratitude for their friendship and her regret over the mistake.

Tears welled up in Lucy's eyes as she flipped through the pages.

She saw the effort Emma had put into each drawing and felt a pang of guilt for not giving her friend a chance to explain. She realized that true friendship was about understanding and forgiveness.

"Emma, I'm sorry too," Lucy said, her voice trembling. "I should have believed you and given you a chance to explain. I miss our friendship."

Emma's eyes filled with tears as well. "I miss it too, Lucy. Can we start over?"

Lucy nodded and hugged Emma tightly. "Yes, we can. Let's put this behind us."

From that day on, Lucy and Emma worked hard to rebuild their friendship. Emma published a heartfelt apology in the school newspaper, and Lucy's art received the praise it deserved. They learned that forgiveness wasn't always easy, but it was essential for their bond to grow stronger.

As they walked home together, Emma said, "You know, this whole thing taught me something important."

"What's that?" Lucy asked, curious.

"That friendship is like art. It requires patience, understanding, and sometimes, a little forgiveness," Emma replied with a smile.

Lucy smiled back, feeling a sense of peace. "I couldn't agree more, Emma. Thank you for being my friend."

And so, Lucy and Emma's friendship became even stronger, built on a foundation of trust, understanding, and the art of forgiveness.

Betrayed

- Definition: To be hurt by someone's actions, especially when they break your trust.
- Sample: Lucy felt betrayed by Emma's mistaken words in the newspaper article, which criticized her art instead of praising it.

Confront

- Definition: To face someone in a direct and challenging way, especially to deal with a problem or disagreement.
- Sample: Lucy decided to confront Emma about the article to express her hurt feelings and seek an explanation.

Tension

- Definition: A feeling of nervousness or unease between people, often because of a disagreement or lack of trust.
- Sample: After the misunderstanding, tension grew between Lucy and Emma, causing them to avoid each other at school.

Regret

- Definition: A feeling of sadness or disappointment about something that you have done or that has happened.
- Sample: Emma felt deep regret for the typo in the newspaper that hurt Lucy and strained their friendship.

Apology

- Definition: A statement in which you express regret for having done or said something wrong.
- Sample: Emma published a heartfelt apology in the school newspaper, expressing her sincere regret for the mistake she made about Lucy's art.

Gratitude

- Definition: The quality of being thankful; readiness to show appreciation for and to return kindness.

- Sample: Emma expressed her gratitude to Lucy through the sketches of their favorite memories together, hoping to mend their broken friendship.

Bridge

- Definition: To make a connection between two people or groups who have disagreed or been apart.
- Sample: Lucy and Emma worked hard to bridge the gap caused by the misunderstanding, eventually rebuilding their friendship.

Patience

- Definition: The ability to wait, or to continue doing something despite difficulties, without becoming annoyed or anxious.
- Sample: Rebuilding their friendship required patience from both Lucy and Emma as they worked through their hurt feelings and misunderstandings.

Foundation

- Definition: The solid base on which something is built; a basis or groundwork.
- Sample: Lucy and Emma's renewed friendship was built on a strong foundation of trust, understanding, and forgiveness.

9.

A DAY IN THE LIFE
OF A DOCTOR

Dr. Sarah Smith woke up early, as usual, before the sun had even risen. She stretched, yawned, and rolled out of bed, knowing she had a busy day ahead at the hospital. She quickly got dressed, grabbed a quick breakfast, and headed out the door.

On her way to work, she thought about the patients she had seen the previous day. There was Mrs. Thompson, who had come in with a high fever, and Mr. Lee, who was recovering from surgery. Dr. Smith felt a sense of duty and responsibility towards her patients, always wanting to do her best to help them.

As she arrived at the hospital, she greeted the nurses at the front desk. "Good morning, everyone!"

"Good morning, Dr. Smith!" they replied in unison, with smiles on their faces.

Dr. Smith made her way to her office, where she checked her schedule for the day. She had several appointments lined up, as well as a few surgeries to perform. It was going to be a long day, but she was ready for it.

Her first patient was a young boy named Timmy, who had come in with a broken arm. Dr. Smith examined the X-rays and saw that the break was clean and would heal well with a cast. She gently explained the procedure to Timmy and his worried mother.

"Don't worry, Timmy," she said with a reassuring smile. "You'll be as good as new in no time."

Timmy looked up at her with wide eyes and nodded bravely. Dr. Smith carefully set the bone and wrapped his arm in a bright blue cast. Timmy chose the color himself and seemed pleased with his decision.

After seeing a few more patients, Dr. Smith headed to the operating room for her first surgery of the day. She changed into her surgical scrubs and scrubbed her hands thoroughly. The surgery was a complicated one, but Dr. Smith remained focused and calm throughout. Her years of experience and steady hands helped her perform the surgery successfully.

Once the surgery was complete, she spoke with the patient's family, explaining how the procedure had gone and answering their questions. The relief on their faces made all the hard work worthwhile.

Back in her office, Dr. Smith took a quick break to eat lunch. She chatted with her colleague, Dr. Brown, who was also taking a break.

"How's your day going?" Dr. Brown asked.

"Busy as always," Dr. Smith replied with a chuckle. "But I wouldn't have it any other way."

Dr. Brown nodded in agreement. "Same here. It's demanding, but it's also very rewarding."

After lunch, Dr. Smith continued with her appointments. She saw a variety of patients with different ailments, from the common cold to more serious conditions. She listened carefully to each patient, making sure to address their concerns and provide the best possible care.

One of her afternoon patients was an elderly woman named

Mrs. Jenkins, who came in for a routine check-up. Mrs. Jenkins was a regular patient, and Dr. Smith always enjoyed their chats.

"How are you feeling today, Mrs. Jenkins?" Dr. Smith asked as she took her blood pressure.

"Oh, you know, the usual aches and pains," Mrs. Jenkins replied with a smile. "But I can't complain."

Dr. Smith laughed softly. "Well, let's make sure everything is in order."

After the check-up, Dr. Smith prescribed some medication for Mrs. Jenkins' arthritis and advised her on some exercises to help with the pain.

As the day drew to a close, Dr. Smith reviewed her notes and prepared for her final appointment. It was a follow-up with Mr. Lee, who had undergone surgery a week earlier. She was pleased to see that he was recovering well and that his condition had improved significantly.

"Thank you, Dr. Smith," Mr. Lee said gratefully. "I feel much better now."

"You're welcome, Mr. Lee. Just make sure to follow the instructions and take it easy for a while," Dr. Smith advised.

Finally, with all her patients seen and her paperwork completed, Dr. Smith headed home. She felt tired but satisfied with the day's work. She knew she had made a difference in her patients' lives, and that thought always brought her a sense of fulfillment.

As she drove home, she reflected on her career choice. Being a doctor was not easy, but it was her passion. She loved the challenge, the problem-solving, and most of all, the opportunity to help people.

Dr. Smith arrived home, greeted by her dog, Max, who wagged

his tail excitedly. She spent the evening relaxing, reading a book, and enjoying a well-deserved dinner. She knew that tomorrow would bring another busy day, but she was ready for it.

With a smile on her face, Dr. Smith went to bed, knowing she had given her best and made a positive impact on her patients. And that was enough to make her feel grateful and content.

Routine

- Definition: A sequence of actions regularly followed; a fixed program.
- Sample: Dr. Smith's morning routine included waking up early, getting dressed quickly, and grabbing breakfast before heading to the hospital.

Responsibility

- Definition: The state or fact of having a duty to deal with something or of having control over someone.
- Sample: Dr. Smith felt a strong sense of responsibility towards her patients, always striving to provide them with the best care possible.

Reassuring

- Definition: Providing comfort or confidence to someone.
- Sample: Dr. Smith reassured Timmy and his mother that his broken arm would heal well with a cast, putting their worries at ease.

Procedure

- Definition: A series of actions conducted in a certain order or manner.
- Sample: Dr. Smith carefully explained the procedure for setting Timmy's broken arm and applying the cast, ensuring both Timmy and his mother understood.

Complicated

- Definition: Involving many different and confusing aspects.
- Sample: The surgery Dr. Smith performed that day was complicated, requiring her to remain focused and calm throughout the procedure.

Successful

- Definition: Achieving the desired results or having a favorable outcome.
- Sample: Dr. Smith's surgery was successful, and she was able to speak with the patient's family afterward to explain how it went.

Colleague

- Definition: A person with whom one works in the same profession or organization.
- Sample: Dr. Smith chatted with her colleague, Dr. Brown, during lunch, sharing experiences and discussing their busy days.

Ailment

- Definition: An illness, typically a minor one.
- Sample: Throughout the day, Dr. Smith saw patients with various ailments, from common colds to more serious conditions.

Chats

- Definition: Informal conversations.
- Sample: Dr. Smith enjoyed her chats with Mrs. Jenkins during her routine check-ups, where they would catch up and discuss her health.

Gratefully

- Definition: Feeling or showing appreciation or thanks.

- Sample: Mr. Lee thanked Dr. Smith gratefully after his follow-up appointment, expressing his appreciation for her care and advice.

10.

THE MAGIC PEN

Lucy was a curious and imaginative girl who loved to draw. Every day after school, she would sit at her small wooden desk by the window, drawing pictures of magical lands and fantastic creatures. One rainy afternoon, she found herself at the local antique shop with her grandmother.

As they wandered through the dusty aisles, Lucy's eyes caught sight of an old wooden box. It was tucked away on a high shelf, almost hidden from view. "Grandma, can we look at that box?" Lucy asked, pointing up.

Her grandmother nodded and helped her reach the box. It was beautifully carved with intricate patterns, and inside, nestled in a bed of velvet, lay a simple, yet elegant, silver pen.

"Can I have it, Grandma?" Lucy asked, her eyes wide with excitement.

Her grandmother smiled. "Of course, my dear. It looks like it was meant for you."

Back at home, Lucy couldn't wait to try out her new pen. She opened her sketchbook and began to draw a picture of a small bird. As soon as she finished the drawing, something incredible happened. The bird slowly lifted off the page, flapped its wings, and started to fly around her room.

Lucy gasped in amazement. "This pen is magic!" she exclaimed. She watched in awe as the bird landed gently on her shoulder, chirping softly.

Over the next few days, Lucy experimented with the magic

pen. She drew a beautiful butterfly, which fluttered around her head, and a playful kitten that chased the butterfly across her room. Each drawing came to life in the most vivid and wonderful way.

One evening, Lucy decided to draw a grand adventure. She drew herself standing in front of a majestic castle, with knights, dragons, and a treasure hidden deep inside. As soon as she finished, she found herself transported into the drawing. She was standing at the gates of the castle, feeling both excited and a little nervous.

"Hello?" she called out, her voice echoing off the stone walls.

A knight in shining armor approached her. "Welcome, brave Lucy," he said. "We have been waiting for you. The kingdom is in need of your help."

Lucy followed the knight into the castle, where the king and queen were seated on their thrones. "We have heard of your magical pen," the king said. "Our kingdom is in danger, and only you can save it."

Lucy felt a surge of determination. "What do I need to do?" she asked.

The queen handed her a blank scroll. "Draw the creature that is causing trouble in our kingdom," she said. "And then draw a way to defeat it."

Lucy took out her magic pen and began to draw. She sketched a fierce dragon, its eyes glowing with menace. The dragon roared to life, but Lucy was not afraid. She quickly drew a brave knight, armed with a magical sword. The knight charged at the dragon, and after an intense battle, the dragon was defeated.

The kingdom erupted in cheers. "Thank you, Lucy," the king said. "You have saved us all."

Lucy smiled, feeling proud of her accomplishment. "I'm happy

I could help," she said.

With a flash of light, Lucy found herself back in her room. The drawing of the castle and the adventure was still in her sketchbook, but now it was just a picture again. She looked around her room at all the other drawings she had made with the magic pen. The butterfly was resting on her windowsill, the kitten was curled up on her bed, and the bird was perched on her desk.

"Wow," Lucy said to herself. "This pen really is magic."

From that day on, Lucy used the pen to create many more adventures. She shared her drawings with her friends and family, bringing a little bit of magic into their lives as well. Whenever someone needed cheering up, Lucy would draw something special for them, and it would always come to life and bring joy.

One day, as Lucy was drawing in the park, a little boy approached her. He looked sad and lonely. "Hi," Lucy said kindly. "Would you like to see something amazing?"

The boy nodded, his eyes curious. Lucy took out her magic pen and drew a friendly puppy. The puppy sprang to life, wagging its tail and licking the boy's hand. The boy's face lit up with a big smile.

"Thank you!" he exclaimed, hugging the puppy.

Lucy felt a warm glow in her heart. She realized that the magic pen wasn't just about creating wonderful things for herself, but about sharing that magic with others. From that day on, she made it her mission to use the pen to help and bring happiness to as many people as possible.

Lucy learned that true magic lies not just in what we create, but in the joy and kindness we share with others. And with her magic pen, she knew she could make the world a brighter, more magical place.

Intricate

- o   Definition: Very detailed or complex.
- o   Sample: The old wooden box had intricate patterns carved into its surface, showcasing skilled craftsmanship.

Nestled

- o   Definition: Settled or nestled comfortably or snugly.
- o   Sample: Inside the box, the silver pen was nestled in a bed of velvet, waiting to be discovered by Lucy.

Vivid

- o   Definition: Producing very clear and detailed images in the mind; intensely bright or colorful.
- o   Sample: Each drawing Lucy made with the magic pen came to life in the most vivid and wonderful way, filling her room with animated creatures.

Majestic

- o   Definition: Having or showing impressive beauty or dignity.
- o   Sample: Lucy drew herself standing in front of a majestic castle, surrounded by knights and dragons, in her grand adventure drawing.

Determination

- o   Definition: Firmness of purpose; resoluteness.
- o   Sample: Lucy felt a surge of determination when tasked with saving the kingdom, knowing she had to use her magic pen wisely.

Menace

- o   Definition: A person or thing that is likely to cause harm; a threat or danger.

o   Sample: The dragon Lucy drew had glowing eyes filled with menace, posing a threat to the kingdom in her adventure drawing.

Accomplishment

o   Definition: Something that has been achieved successfully; a goal reached.

o   Sample: Lucy felt proud of her accomplishment after defeating the dragon and saving the kingdom, knowing she had made a significant difference.

Curled up

o   Definition: Sit or lie down comfortably, with the limbs close to the body and the back rounded.

o   Sample: The playful kitten Lucy drew was curled up on her bed, content after chasing the butterfly across the room.

Erupted

o   Definition: To break out suddenly and dramatically.

o   Sample: The kingdom erupted in cheers after Lucy's brave knight defeated the dragon, celebrating their newfound safety and peace.

Mission

o   Definition: An important assignment carried out for political, religious, or commercial purposes, typically involving travel.

o   Sample: Lucy made it her mission to use the magic pen to bring happiness and joy to as many people as possible, realizing its potential to spread magic and kindness.

11.

A JOURNEY TO
THE PAST

Jake had always been fascinated by history. He loved reading books and watching documentaries about different periods. But his favorite subject was his family history. He often wondered what life was like for his ancestors and what stories they had to tell.

One sunny afternoon, Jake was visiting his grandmother. She had a large, old house filled with memories and antiques. Jake loved exploring her attic, where she kept many of the family's old belongings. Today, he was on a mission to find a particular object his grandmother had mentioned—a pocket watch that belonged to his great-great-grandfather.

As he rummaged through dusty boxes, Jake finally found the watch. It was beautiful, with intricate engravings and a heavy, solid feel. When he opened it, he noticed an inscription: "To George, time is a gift. Use it wisely."

"Wow," Jake whispered to himself. As he held the watch, he felt a strange sensation, as if the room were spinning. Suddenly, everything went dark.

When Jake opened his eyes, he found himself in a completely different place. The modern attic was gone, replaced by a small, dimly lit room with wooden furniture and old-fashioned decorations. He looked around in confusion. "Where am I?" he thought.

The door opened, and a man walked in. He wore old-fashioned clothes and had a kind face. "Hello," the man said, looking just as surprised as Jake. "Who are you?"

Jake took a deep breath. "I'm Jake. I think I might have traveled back in time."

The man raised an eyebrow but didn't seem too shocked. "I'm George," he said. "Welcome to my home."

Jake's eyes widened. "George? Are you my great-great-grandfather?"

George looked thoughtful. "I don't know about that, but you are certainly a stranger in these parts. How did you get here?"

Jake showed him the pocket watch. "I found this watch in my grandmother's attic. When I opened it, I ended up here."

George examined the watch closely. "This is my watch. I don't know how it brought you here, but it seems you have traveled through time."

Jake couldn't believe it. He had always dreamed of something like this happening, but now that it had, he didn't know what to do. "Can you tell me about your life?" he asked. "I've always wanted to know more about my ancestors."

George smiled. "Of course. Come, sit with me."

They sat by the fireplace, and George began to share his stories. He talked about his life as a blacksmith, the challenges he faced, and the joys he found in his work. He spoke of his family, the community, and the values they held dear. Jake listened intently, absorbing every detail.

"Life was tough," George said, "but we found happiness in simple things. We worked hard, helped each other, and always made time for family."

Jake nodded. "It sounds different from today. We have so

much technology, but sometimes it feels like we're more disconnected."

George looked thoughtful. "Every time has its challenges and its blessings. It's important to remember what's truly valuable —family, friends, and the time we spend together."

Jake felt a deep sense of gratitude for this unexpected journey. He realized that his great-great-grandfather's words held timeless wisdom. "Thank you for sharing your stories with me," he said.

George smiled. "Thank you for listening. I believe it's time for you to return to your own time."

Jake looked at the pocket watch in his hand. He wasn't sure how to activate it, but he closed his eyes and concentrated on home. The strange sensation returned, and when he opened his eyes, he was back in the attic.

Everything was as it had been before, but Jake felt different. He had gained a new perspective and a deeper appreciation for his family's history. He knew he had to share what he had learned with his grandmother and the rest of his family.

Jake hurried downstairs to find his grandmother. "Grandma, you won't believe what just happened!" he exclaimed.

She looked at him with a knowing smile. "You found the watch, didn't you?"

Jake nodded, amazed. "Did you know it could do that?"

"I had heard stories," she said. "But I never experienced it myself. I'm glad you had the chance to meet George."

Jake spent the rest of the afternoon sharing his adventure with his grandmother. She listened with great interest, adding her own stories and memories. Together, they realized that understanding the past could bring them closer to each other and help them appreciate the present.

That night, as Jake lay in bed, he thought about his journey to the past. He felt grateful for the experience and the lessons he had learned. He understood now that history wasn't just about dates and events—it was about people, their lives, and the values they passed down through generations.

Jake decided to keep the pocket watch in a special place and promised himself to use his time wisely, just as his great-great-grandfather had advised. He knew that the stories of the past would always be with him, guiding him as he created his own future.

Intricate

- Definition: Very detailed or complicated; having many small parts or patterns.
- Sample: The pocket watch Jake found in his grandmother's attic was beautifully intricate, with delicate engravings and tiny gears visible through the glass casing.

Dimly

- Definition: With a faint or subdued light; not brightly.
- Sample: Jake found himself in a dimly lit room after he traveled back in time, surrounded by old-fashioned wooden furniture and muted colors.

Absorbing

- Definition: Very interesting and engaging; holding one's attention completely.
- Sample: Jake listened intently to his great-great-grandfather's stories, absorbing every detail about life as a blacksmith in the past.

Unexpected

- Definition: Not expected; surprising or unforeseen.
- Sample: Jake's journey back in time was unexpected, triggered by the opening of the old pocket watch found in his grandmother's attic.

Timeless

- Definition: Not affected by the passage of time; eternal or enduring.
- Sample: The wisdom shared by Jake's great-great-grandfather about family and values was timeless, resonating with Jake despite the centuries between them.

Gratitude

- Definition: The quality of being thankful; readiness to show appreciation for and to return kindness.
- Sample: Jake felt a deep sense of gratitude towards his great-great-grandfather for sharing his life stories and wisdom during their brief encounter in the past.

Perspective

- Definition: A particular attitude or way of regarding something; a point of view.
- Sample: Jake gained a new perspective on history and family after his journey to the past, realizing the importance of understanding his ancestors' lives.

Appreciation

- Definition: Recognition and enjoyment of the good qualities of someone or something.
- Sample: Jake gained a deeper appreciation for his family's history and values after hearing firsthand accounts from his great-great-grandfather.

Guiding

- Definition: Showing the way; directing or influencing in

a particular direction.

- Sample: The lessons Jake learned from his great-great-grandfather's stories about hard work and family values would continue to guide him throughout his life.

Promise

- Definition: A declaration or assurance that one will do something or that a particular thing will happen.
- Sample: Jake promised himself to use his time wisely, inspired by the inscription on the pocket watch and the lessons learned from his journey to the past.

12.

THE MISSING NECKLACE

It was a beautiful evening, and Olivia was excited about the party at her friend Emma's house. Emma always threw the best parties, and this one promised to be even more special because it was her birthday. Olivia put on her favorite dress and the necklace her grandmother had given her. It was a delicate silver chain with a small, sparkling pendant. It was her most valuable possession, and she felt lucky to wear it.

When Olivia arrived at the party, the house was already buzzing with music and laughter. She greeted Emma with a big hug and handed her a beautifully wrapped gift. "Happy birthday, Emma! I hope you like it."

Emma smiled and took the gift. "Thank you, Olivia! I'm sure I will. Come on in, and let's have some fun."

The party was in full swing. There were lots of people, delicious food, and a lively atmosphere. Olivia joined her friends on the dance floor and enjoyed herself, forgetting all her worries. After a while, she went to the kitchen to get a drink.

As she poured herself some juice, she noticed a group of people gathered around the dining table, talking excitedly. Curious, she walked over to see what was going on. Emma was standing in the middle, looking worried.

"What's happening?" Olivia asked, concerned.

Emma sighed. "My necklace is missing. It was a birthday present from my parents, and it's very valuable. I had it on earlier, but now it's gone."

Olivia's heart sank. She understood how Emma felt because her own necklace was so precious to her. "I'm so sorry, Emma. Is there anything I can do to help?"

Emma nodded. "We're trying to figure out what happened. Maybe you can ask around and see if anyone saw anything?"

Olivia agreed and began talking to the guests. Most people hadn't noticed anything unusual, but one of Emma's friends, Jake, mentioned something interesting.

"I saw someone near the dining table a while ago," Jake said. "I think it was a woman in a red dress. She was looking at the jewelry on display."

Olivia thanked Jake and continued her search. She found the woman in the red dress, whose name was Clara, talking to a group of friends. Olivia approached her and explained the situation.

Clara looked surprised. "Oh, I remember seeing the necklace. It was beautiful. But I didn't take it, I swear. I was just admiring it."

Olivia believed her. Clara seemed sincere, and there was no reason to doubt her. But if Clara didn't take the necklace, who did? Olivia was determined to solve the mystery.

She decided to retrace her steps. She went back to the kitchen and then to the dining table, looking carefully around. Suddenly, something caught her eye—a small, shiny object under the table. She bent down and picked it up. It was a silver clasp, just like the one on Emma's necklace.

Excited, Olivia showed the clasp to Emma. "Look, I found this under the table. Do you think it's from your necklace?"

Emma examined it closely. "Yes, it is! How did it get there?"

Olivia thought for a moment. "Maybe the necklace fell off while you were dancing or moving around. It could have slipped off without you noticing."

Emma nodded. "That makes sense. But where is the rest of the necklace?"

They decided to search the area around the dining table more thoroughly. After a few minutes, Olivia spotted something glittering behind a chair. She reached out and picked up the missing necklace. "I found it!" she exclaimed, holding it up for Emma to see.

Emma's face lit up with relief. "Oh, thank you, Olivia! You saved my birthday. I was so worried I had lost it forever."

Olivia smiled. "I'm just glad we found it. It's such a special gift. I know how much it means to you."

Emma hugged Olivia tightly. "You're a great friend. I don't know what I would have done without you."

The rest of the party went smoothly. Emma put her necklace back on, and everyone continued to enjoy the evening. Olivia felt happy and proud that she had helped her friend. She realized that sometimes, a little bit of effort and determination could make a big difference.

As the night drew to a close, Olivia said goodbye to Emma and headed home. She thought about the evening's events and smiled. It had been a memorable night, not just because of the party, but because she had learned the value of friendship and the importance of helping others.

When Olivia got home, she carefully took off her own necklace and placed it in its special box. She knew that while the necklace was valuable, the memories and connections it represented were even more precious. And that was something worth cherishing forever.

Delicate - Easily broken or damaged; fragile.

- o   Olivia wore a delicate silver chain with a small, sparkling pendant.

Possession - Something owned; a belonging.

- o   The necklace was Olivia's most valuable possession.

Buzzing - Making a low, continuous humming sound.

- o   The house was already buzzing with music and laughter.

Concerned - Worried or anxious.

- o   "What's happening?" Olivia asked, concerned.

Valuable - Worth a lot of money or important.

- o   The necklace was a valuable birthday present from Emma's parents.

Precious - Of great value; not to be wasted or treated carelessly.

- o   Olivia's own necklace was very precious to her.

Excitedly - With enthusiasm or eagerness.

- o   People were gathered around the dining table, talking excitedly.

Curious - Eager to know or learn something.

- o   Curious, Olivia walked over to see what was going on.

Sincere - Free from pretense or deceit; genuine.

- o   Clara seemed sincere when she denied taking the necklace.

Determined - Having made a firm decision and being resolved not to change it.

   o   Olivia was determined to solve the mystery of the missing necklace.

Thoroughly - In a thorough manner; completely.

   o   They decided to search the area around the dining table more thoroughly.

Glittering - Shining with a bright, shimmering light.

   o   Olivia spotted something glittering behind a chair.

Relief - A feeling of reassurance and relaxation following release from anxiety or distress.

   o   Emma's face lit up with relief when the necklace was found.

Effort - A vigorous or determined attempt.

   o   Olivia realized that sometimes, a little bit of effort could make a big difference.

Memorable - Worth remembering or easily remembered.

   o   It had been a memorable night, not just because of the party.

13.

THE BOOKSTORE CAT

In a quiet corner of the city, there was a small, charming bookstore called "The Book Nook." This bookstore was special for many reasons, but the most unique thing about it was its friendly resident cat, Whiskers. Whiskers was a fluffy, orange tabby with a playful personality and a knack for making everyone feel welcome.

One sunny morning, Emily, the owner of The Book Nook, unlocked the door and let Whiskers out of his little bed behind the counter. "Good morning, Whiskers," she said, scratching behind his ears. "Ready to help our customers today?"

Whiskers meowed in response, as if to say, "Of course!" He stretched and then made his way to his favorite spot by the window. From there, he could see the people passing by and watch the world go by.

The first customer of the day was Mr. Thompson, an elderly man who loved mystery novels. He had been a regular at the bookstore for years. Whiskers recognized him immediately and jumped off the windowsill to greet him. Mr. Thompson chuckled as Whiskers rubbed against his legs.

"Good morning, Emily," Mr. Thompson said, smiling. "And good morning to you too, Whiskers. Do you have any new mysteries for me today?"

Emily nodded and pointed to a new display near the back of the store. "We just got a shipment of new releases yesterday. I'm sure you'll find something you like."

As Mr. Thompson browsed the shelves, Whiskers followed him, occasionally batting at a dangling bookmark or purring loudly. Mr. Thompson enjoyed the cat's company and often spoke to him as he shopped. "What do you think, Whiskers? Should I read this one next?" Whiskers would respond with a soft meow, and Mr. Thompson would laugh.

Later in the morning, a young woman named Lisa entered the store. She was new to the neighborhood and looking for a good book to read. She was immediately charmed by the cozy atmosphere of The Book Nook and, of course, by Whiskers.

"Hello," Lisa said to Emily. "This place is lovely. And what a beautiful cat!"

Emily smiled. "Thank you! That's Whiskers. He loves to help our customers. What kind of book are you looking for today?"

Lisa thought for a moment. "I'm not sure. Maybe something uplifting and inspiring."

Emily nodded and led Lisa to a section filled with motivational and self-help books. Whiskers trotted alongside them, occasionally stopping to sniff a book or sit beside Lisa as she picked up different titles. Lisa found herself feeling more relaxed and happy just being around Whiskers.

"He's so friendly," Lisa remarked, petting Whiskers gently. "I've never seen a cat like him in a bookstore before."

"He's special," Emily agreed. "Whiskers has been with us since we opened. He has a way of knowing what people need. Sometimes, it feels like he's the real owner of this place."

Lisa laughed. "Well, he's certainly doing a great job. I think I'll take this one." She held up a book with a bright cover that promised to bring joy and positivity into her life.

As the day went on, more customers came and went. There was a group of children from a nearby school, excited to pick out new stories to read. Whiskers played with them, chasing a piece of string they dangled in front of him. There was also a young couple looking for a cookbook to try new recipes together. Whiskers sat on the counter, observing them with interest as they debated which book to choose.

In the afternoon, Emily's friend, Laura, dropped by for a visit. Laura worked at the animal shelter where Emily had adopted Whiskers. "How's our favorite bookstore cat doing?" she asked, scratching Whiskers under his chin.

"He's doing great, as always," Emily replied. "He really brightens up this place."

Laura smiled. "I'm glad to hear that. Whiskers has a special gift. He brings people together and makes them happy."

Emily nodded in agreement. "It's true. People come here for the books, but they stay for Whiskers."

As the sun began to set, the last customer of the day, a man named James, walked in. He looked tired and a bit lost. Emily greeted him with a warm smile. "Welcome to The Book Nook. How can I help you?"

James sighed. "I'm not sure. I've had a rough day and just need something to take my mind off things."

Emily thought for a moment. "Why don't you take a look at our fiction section? Sometimes, a good story can be the perfect escape."

Whiskers seemed to sense James' mood and quietly followed him to the back of the store. James browsed the shelves slowly, eventually picking out a novel with an intriguing cover. As he sat down to read a few pages, Whiskers hopped onto the chair beside him, curling up and purring softly. James couldn't help but smile.

"Thanks, little guy," he whispered, feeling a bit of his stress melt away. "I think I'll take this one."

As James left with his book, Emily watched him go, feeling grateful for Whiskers and the joy he brought to everyone who visited The Book Nook. She knew that her bookstore was special, not just because of the books it held, but because of the warmth and comfort that Whiskers provided.

When it was time to close up, Emily gave Whiskers a final scratch behind the ears. "Good job today, Whiskers. You made a lot of people happy."

Whiskers purred contentedly, ready for another day of helping customers and making new friends. And so, The Book Nook continued to be a place where stories came to life and a friendly cat named Whiskers made everyone feel right at home.

Charming - Pleasant or attractive.

- This bookstore was special for many reasons, but the most unique thing about it was its charming resident cat, Whiskers.

Unique - Being the only one of its kind; unlike anything else.

- The Book Nook was unique because of its friendly resident cat, Whiskers.

Recognized - To know someone or something because you have seen or experienced them before.

- Whiskers recognized Mr. Thompson immediately and jumped off the windowsill to greet him.

Shipment - A batch of goods sent to a place.

- We just got a shipment of new releases yesterday.

Occasionally - At infrequent or irregular intervals; now and then.

- Whiskers followed him, occasionally batting at a dangling bookmark or purring loudly.

Motivational - Providing reasons or encouragement to do something.

- Emily led Lisa to a section filled with motivational and self-help books.

Trotted - To move at a pace faster than a walk, lifting each diagonal pair of legs alternately.

- Whiskers trotted alongside them, occasionally stopping to sniff a book.

Uplifting - Morally or spiritually elevating; inspiring happiness or hope.

- Maybe something uplifting and inspiring, Lisa thought.

Relaxed - Free from tension and anxiety; at ease.

- Lisa found herself feeling more relaxed and happy just being around Whiskers.

Debated - To argue about (a subject), especially in a formal manner.

- Whiskers observed them with interest as they debated which book to choose.

Brightens - Makes or becomes lighter, more cheerful, or more likely to bring happiness.

- He really brightens up this place, Emily said.

Gift - A natural ability or talent.

- Whiskers has a special gift. He brings people together and makes them happy.

Grateful - Feeling or showing an appreciation for something done or received.

- Emily felt grateful for Whiskers and the joy he brought to everyone who visited The Book Nook.

Eventually - In the end, especially after a long delay, dispute, or series of events.

- James browsed the shelves slowly, eventually picking out a novel with an intriguing cover.

Contentedly - Happily at ease.

- Whiskers purred contentedly, ready for another day of helping customers and making new friends.

14.

THE SILENT HERO

Sam was the janitor at a large office building in the city. He had worked there for many years and knew every corner of the place. His job was not glamorous, but he took pride in keeping everything clean and running smoothly. The people in the building often overlooked him, but Sam didn't mind. He enjoyed his work and found satisfaction in the small, everyday tasks that made a big difference.

One Monday morning, the office was busier than usual. The company that occupied the top floors was preparing for a major presentation. Important clients were coming from out of town, and the entire team was in a frenzy, making sure everything was perfect. Sam could feel the tension in the air as he went about his duties.

While mopping the floors in the lobby, Sam overheard a conversation between two employees, Lisa and Mark. They were discussing the presentation.

"Everything has to be perfect," Lisa said, looking worried. "If this presentation doesn't go well, we could lose the client."

Mark nodded. "I know. I've double-checked everything, but I'm still nervous. The projector in the conference room was acting up yesterday. I hope it works today."

Sam made a mental note of this as he continued his work. He had seen the team in the conference room the day before, struggling with the projector. He decided to check it out himself once he finished his tasks.

Later, when the office was quieter, Sam went to the conference room. The projector was a crucial part of the presentation, and he knew how important it was for everything to go smoothly. He carefully examined the projector and discovered that the problem was a loose wire. Using his toolkit, he fixed the wire and tested the projector to make sure it was working perfectly.

Just as he was finishing up, he heard footsteps behind him. It was Lisa. She looked surprised to see him there.

"Sam, what are you doing?" she asked.

"I heard there was a problem with the projector," Sam replied, smiling. "I thought I'd take a look and see if I could help."

Lisa's face lit up with relief. "Oh, thank you, Sam! I was so worried about it. Did you fix it?"

Sam nodded. "Yes, it should be working fine now. Just make sure to test it again before the presentation."

"You're a lifesaver," Lisa said, genuinely grateful. "I don't know what we would have done without you."

Sam just smiled and went back to his work. He didn't need recognition or praise; he was happy knowing he had helped.

As the day went on, the office buzzed with activity. The clients arrived, and the presentation began. Everything went smoothly, and the team impressed the clients with their professionalism and creativity. Lisa and Mark both felt a huge sense of relief and pride.

After the clients left, the office celebrated. The team gathered in the break room, chatting excitedly about how well everything had gone. Lisa raised her glass of sparkling water and made a toast.

"I just want to say thank you to everyone for all your hard work," she said. "And a special thank you to Sam, who quietly saved the day by fixing the projector."

The room erupted in applause. Sam, who was standing near the back, felt a little embarrassed but also proud. It was rare for him to be the center of attention, but he appreciated the kind words.

Mark walked over to Sam and shook his hand. "Thanks again, Sam. You really helped us out today."

"No problem," Sam replied modestly. "I'm just glad I could help."

As the celebration continued, Sam slipped out of the break room and returned to his duties. There were still floors to mop and trash to empty, and he liked to keep busy.

The next day, as Sam arrived at work, he noticed something different. There was a sign on the office door with his name on it. It read, "Thank you, Sam, our Silent Hero." Underneath, there were signatures from all the employees, along with messages of thanks.

Sam felt a lump in his throat as he read the sign. He had never expected such recognition, and it touched him deeply. He went about his work that day with a spring in his step, knowing that his efforts were appreciated.

From that day on, the people in the office made a point to greet Sam and thank him for his hard work. They realized that, while his role might seem small, it was essential to the smooth running of their daily operations. Sam continued to do his job with quiet dedication, knowing that even the smallest acts of kindness and service could make a big difference.

In the end, Sam remained the silent hero of the office, always there to lend a hand and keep things running smoothly. His story became a reminder to everyone that sometimes, the most important contributions come from those who work quietly behind the scenes.

Janitor - A person employed to clean and maintain a building.

o Sam was the janitor at a large office building in the city.

Glamorous - Having an attractive or exciting quality.

o His job was not glamorous, but he took pride in keeping everything clean.

Frenzy - A state of intense excitement or activity.

o The entire team was in a frenzy, making sure everything was perfect.

Presentation - A talk or display given to an audience.

o The company was preparing for a major presentation.

Crucial - Extremely important or necessary.

o The projector was a crucial part of the presentation.

Examined - To inspect or look at closely.

o He carefully examined the projector and discovered that the problem was a loose wire.

Lifesaver - A person or thing that saves someone from a difficult situation.

o "You're a lifesaver," Lisa said, genuinely grateful.

Recognition - Acknowledgment of someone's effort or achievement.

o He didn't need recognition or praise; he was happy knowing he had helped.

Professionally - In a manner that is appropriate for the workplace; with skill and competence.

- ○ The team impressed the clients with their professionalism and creativity.

Genuine - Sincere and honest.

- ○ Lisa's face lit up with genuine relief when Sam fixed the projector.

Modestly - In a humble or unassuming manner.

- ○ "No problem," Sam replied modestly. "I'm just glad I could help."

Dedication - The quality of being committed to a task or purpose.

- ○ Sam continued to do his job with quiet dedication.

Recognition - The acknowledgment of someone's achievement.

- ○ There was a sign on the office door with his name on it, showing recognition for his efforts.

Appreciated - Recognized the value or worth of something.

- ○ He liked to keep busy, knowing that his efforts were appreciated.

Contributions - The act of giving or doing something for a common purpose.

- ○ Sometimes, the most important contributions come from those who work quietly behind the scenes.

15.

A NEW BEGINNING

Moving to a new country was both exciting and scary for the Ramirez family. Maria, Carlos, and their two children, Sofia and Mateo, packed their belongings and said goodbye to their home in Mexico. They were moving to Canada for a better life, but they knew it would be hard at first.

"Are you ready, kids?" Maria asked as they waited at the airport.

"Yes, Mom," Sofia said with a smile. She was thirteen and always tried to stay positive.

"I'm a little nervous," admitted Mateo, who was ten years old.

"That's normal," Carlos reassured his son. "We are all feeling a bit nervous. But we have each other, and that's what matters."

When they arrived in Canada, everything felt different. The air was colder, and people spoke English everywhere. Maria and Carlos had learned some English, but it was still hard to understand everyone.

The first challenge was finding a place to live. They stayed in a small apartment at first. It wasn't very big, but it was cozy, and Maria made it feel like home by adding some colorful decorations from Mexico.

"We'll find a bigger place soon," Carlos promised as he unpacked their things. "For now, let's focus on settling in."

The children started school the following week. Sofia was placed in an English class for beginners. She was nervous but also excited to make new friends. Mateo, on the other hand, found it hard at first. He missed his old friends and felt out of place.

"I don't understand anything the teacher says," Mateo said sadly after his first day.

"That's okay, Mateo," Maria comforted him. "It will get easier. Remember, everyone here was new at some point."

Carlos found a job at a local factory. It was hard work, but he was happy to have a job. Maria started taking English classes at a nearby community center while also looking after the children and the apartment.

One day, Maria met a woman named Linda at the community center. Linda was a volunteer who helped new immigrants learn English. She became a good friend to Maria.

"You're doing great, Maria," Linda said one day after class. "It's normal to feel overwhelmed, but you're making progress."

Maria smiled. "Thank you, Linda. Your support means a lot to me."

As the weeks went by, Sofia started to enjoy school more. She joined a soccer team and made friends with some of the other girls. Mateo also began to feel more comfortable. His teacher, Mrs. Green, noticed he was struggling and offered extra help after school.

"You're doing better, Mateo," Mrs. Green said one day. "You should be proud of yourself."

"Thank you, Mrs. Green," Mateo replied, feeling a bit more confident.

The Ramirez family celebrated their first Christmas in Canada. It was different from what they were used to, but they enjoyed it. They invited Linda and some new friends over for a small party. It was a mix of Mexican and Canadian traditions, which made it special.

JOURNEY TO ENGLISH FLUENCY: 50 SHORT STORIES FOR B2 LEVEL LEAR...

"This is nice," Sofia said, looking around at the decorations and smiling faces.

"Yes, it is," Maria agreed. "We're building new memories."

As winter turned to spring, the Ramirez family felt more settled. Carlos's English improved, and he got a promotion at work. Maria's English classes paid off, and she started working part-time at a local bakery. She loved baking and was happy to be working again.

The children also continued to thrive. Sofia's soccer team won a tournament, and she was proud of her achievement. Mateo started to excel in his studies and even helped some of his classmates with their homework.

"Look at us," Carlos said one evening as they sat around the dinner table. "We've come a long way."

"Yes, we have," Maria agreed, looking at her happy children. "It wasn't easy, but we did it together."

One day, the family went to a park for a picnic. They played games, laughed, and enjoyed the beautiful weather. It was a perfect day.

"Remember how scared we were when we first arrived?" Sofia asked.

"Yes," Carlos replied. "But look at us now. We have new friends, new experiences, and we're happy."

"I'm glad we came here," Mateo added. "It's different, but it's good."

Maria looked at her family and felt a wave of gratitude. "We are very lucky," she said. "We have each other, and we have a new beginning. This is home now."

As the sun set, they packed up their things and headed back to their apartment. They knew there would still be challenges ahead, but they also knew they could face them together. Their journey was just beginning, and they were ready for whatever the future held.

Exciting - Causing great enthusiasm and eagerness.

o   Moving to a new country was both exciting and scary for the Ramirez family.

Reassured - Made someone feel less worried or afraid.

o   "That's normal," Carlos reassured his son.

Challenge - A difficult task or problem that requires effort to overcome.

o   The first challenge was finding a place to live.

Cozy - Comfortable and warm.

o   It wasn't very big, but it was cozy, and Maria made it feel like home.

Settling - Establishing oneself in a new place.

o   For now, let's focus on settling in.

Beginners - People who are new to a particular activity or field.

o   Sofia was placed in an English class for beginners.

Missed - Felt the absence of someone or something.

o   Mateo missed his old friends and felt out of place.

Community - A group of people living in the same area or having a particular characteristic in common.

o   Maria started taking English classes at a nearby community center.

Volunteer - A person who offers to do something without

being paid.

- o   Linda was a volunteer who helped new immigrants learn English.

Overwhelmed - Feeling a strong emotional effect from something.

- o   It's normal to feel overwhelmed, but you're making progress.

Progress - Forward movement towards a destination or goal.

- o   You're making progress.

Confident - Feeling sure of oneself and one's abilities.

- o   Mateo replied, feeling a bit more confident.

Promotion - A higher position or rank given as a reward for good performance.

- o   Carlos got a promotion at work.

Thrive - To grow, develop, or be successful.

- o   The children also continued to thrive.

Gratitude - A feeling of thankfulness and appreciation.

- o   Maria looked at her family and felt a wave of gratitude.

16.

THE HAUNTED HOUSE

"Are you sure about this, Tom?" Lisa asked, her voice a mix of excitement and fear. She looked at the old, abandoned house in front of them. The windows were broken, and the paint was peeling off the walls. It looked like something out of a horror movie.

"Yes, I'm sure," Tom replied confidently. "It's just a house. There are no such things as ghosts."

"Easy for you to say," Jack said, nervously adjusting his backpack. "You aren't the one who has to sleep here."

Lisa, Tom, and Jack had been friends since elementary school. They often dared each other to do crazy things, but spending a night in the haunted house was the biggest challenge yet. The house had been empty for years, and everyone in town had a different scary story about it.

The three friends walked up to the front door, which creaked loudly as Tom pushed it open. The inside of the house was dark and dusty. Cobwebs hung from the ceiling, and the floorboards creaked under their feet.

"This place gives me the creeps," Lisa whispered.

"Come on, it's just an old house," Tom said, trying to sound brave. "Let's set up our stuff in the living room."

They walked through the dark hallway and into a large, empty room. The moonlight shone through the broken windows, casting eerie shadows on the walls.

"Perfect spot for a night of fun," Tom said, trying to lighten the mood.

They laid out their sleeping bags and sat in a circle. Tom pulled out a flashlight and some snacks from his backpack.

"Okay, who's ready for ghost stories?" he asked, shining the flashlight under his chin to create a spooky effect.

"Not me," Jack said, looking around nervously. "Why did we have to do this at night? Can't we come back in the morning?"

"Where's the fun in that?" Tom laughed. "We have to do it at night to make it interesting."

Lisa looked around the room. "Do you guys hear that?" she asked suddenly.

"Hear what?" Tom asked, his smile fading.

"It sounded like footsteps," Lisa said, her eyes wide.

"Probably just the wind," Tom said, but even he didn't sound convinced.

They sat in silence for a moment, listening. Then, they heard it again—soft, slow footsteps coming from upstairs.

Jack's face turned pale. "I'm out of here," he said, standing up quickly.

"No, wait," Tom said, grabbing Jack's arm. "Let's check it out. It could be something else."

"Like what?" Jack asked, his voice shaking.

"I don't know, but we're not going to find out by running away," Tom said.

Lisa nodded, trying to be brave. "Let's stick together," she said.

They slowly made their way up the stairs, the old wood creaking with each step. The footsteps grew louder as they reached the top. They followed the sound to a closed door at the end of the hallway.

"Do we really have to open it?" Jack asked, his hand shaking as he reached for the doorknob.

"Yes, we do," Tom said, though his voice wavered.

Jack took a deep breath and turned the doorknob. The door creaked open to reveal a dark room. The three friends stepped inside, holding their breath. Suddenly, a loud crash echoed through the room, and they all screamed.

"It's just a book," Lisa said, picking up an old, dusty book that had fallen from a shelf.

"See? Nothing to be afraid of," Tom said, though he looked relieved.

They turned to leave the room when they heard a voice. "Who are you?" it asked.

They froze in place. "Did you hear that?" Jack whispered.

"Who's there?" Tom called out, his voice trembling.

A figure stepped out from the shadows. It was an old man with a kind face. "I'm sorry if I scared you," he said. "I didn't mean to."

"Who are you?" Lisa asked, her heart still pounding.

"I'm Mr. Johnson," the old man replied. "I used to live here a long time ago. I come back sometimes to check on the place."

"But why at night?" Tom asked, confused.

"Because it's peaceful," Mr. Johnson said with a smile. "No one comes here at night, so it's quiet. I didn't expect to find anyone here."

"We thought the house was haunted," Jack said.

Mr. Johnson laughed. "There are no ghosts here, just memories. This house holds a lot of memories for me."

They spent the rest of the night listening to Mr. Johnson's stories about the house and his life. They learned that the house had been beautiful once, filled with laughter and love. Mr. Johnson's family had lived there for many years before moving away.

By morning, the three friends felt like they had made a new friend. Mr. Johnson thanked them for keeping him company, and they promised to visit him again.

As they left the house, Lisa turned to Tom and Jack. "That was the best night ever," she said.

"Yeah," Jack agreed. "Who knew we'd meet a real-life ghost— well, almost."

Tom smiled. "Sometimes, the scariest places can lead to the best surprises," he said.

They walked back home, feeling braver and more connected than ever. They had faced their fears and made a new friend. It was a night they would never forget.

Abandoned - Left empty or unused for a long period.

o   The old, abandoned house looked like something out of a horror movie.

Challenge - A task or situation that tests someone's abilities.

o   Spending a night in the haunted house was the biggest challenge yet.

Creaked - Made a long, high sound like a door opening or wood bending.

- o   The front door creaked loudly as Tom pushed it open.

Excitement - A feeling of enthusiasm and eagerness.

- o   Lisa's voice was a mix of excitement and fear.

Nervously - In a worried or anxious manner.

- o   Jack nervously adjusted his backpack.

Cobwebs - Spider webs, especially when old and covered in dust.

- o   Cobwebs hung from the ceiling in the dark and dusty house.

Creeps - A feeling of fear or unease.

- o   This place gives me the creeps, Lisa whispered.

Eerie - Strange and frightening.

- o   The moonlight cast eerie shadows on the walls.

Relieved - Feeling reassured and relaxed after being worried.

- o   See? Nothing to be afraid of, Tom said, though he looked relieved.

Trembling - Shaking slightly, usually because of fear or nervousness.

- o   Tom called out, his voice trembling.

Echoed - A sound that is reflected off a surface and heard again.

- o   Suddenly, a loud crash echoed through the room.

Memories - Recollections of past events.

- o   There are no ghosts here, just memories, Mr.

Johnson said.

Peaceful - Free from disturbance; calm.

o   Because it's peaceful, Mr. Johnson said with a smile.

Unexpected - Not expected or predicted.

o   I didn't expect to find anyone here, Mr. Johnson said.

Connected - Joined or linked together.

o   They walked back home, feeling braver and more connected than ever.

17.

THE RECIPE BOOK

It was a rainy Tuesday afternoon when Emma stumbled upon the old recipe book in her grandmother's attic. She had always loved cooking, and the thought of discovering hidden culinary secrets excited her. As she flipped through the yellowed pages, Emma was transported to a different era. Each recipe was a glimpse into the past, written in delicate cursive with notes scribbled in the margins.

"Wow, check this out," Emma called to her roommate, Sarah, who was helping her sort through boxes of old belongings. Sarah joined her on the dusty attic floor, peering over Emma's shoulder at the faded pages of the recipe book.

"What did you find?" Sarah asked, brushing dust off an old chair to sit down.

"It's Grandma's recipe book," Emma replied, her eyes lighting up. "I never knew she had such a treasure hidden away."

Sarah scanned the page Emma was reading. "These recipes look ancient," she remarked, pointing to a recipe for "Grandma's Famous Apple Pie."

"Yeah, but look at the details," Emma said, tracing her finger along the handwritten notes. "She's written about the best type of apples to use and how long to bake it for."

"That's so cool," Sarah said, genuinely impressed. "Do you think you'll try any of these?"

Emma nodded enthusiastically. "Definitely! I want to try them all. It's like unlocking a whole new world of flavors."

Over the next few weeks, Emma immersed herself in the world of Grandma's recipes. She started with simple dishes like hearty stews and comforting soups, using the cookbook as her guide. Each recipe taught her something new—whether it was a cooking technique or a flavor combination she had never considered before.

One rainy Saturday morning, Emma decided to make Grandma's Famous Apple Pie. She followed the recipe meticulously, just as Grandma had written it. The kitchen filled with the scent of cinnamon and baked apples as the pie baked to a golden perfection in the oven.

When it was finally done, Emma couldn't resist taking a bite straight from the oven. The crust was flaky, and the apples were perfectly tender with just the right amount of sweetness. It tasted like home.

As Emma enjoyed her slice of pie, she thought about Grandma and how much joy she must have felt while baking. Emma realized that cooking wasn't just about following a recipe—it was about preserving traditions and creating memories.

Inspired by her newfound passion, Emma decided to share Grandma's recipes with others. She started a blog where she posted photos and stories about each dish she made. People from all over the world began following her journey, trying out the recipes themselves and sharing their own family cooking traditions.

One day, Emma received an email from a local magazine asking her to write a monthly column featuring Grandma's recipes. It was a dream come true for Emma—to turn her hobby into a career sharing her love for cooking with others.

With each new recipe she shared, Emma felt closer to Grandma and the generations of cooks who came before her. The old recipe book had not only changed Emma's career but also enriched her life in ways she never imagined.

As she flipped through the pages of the recipe book one evening, Emma couldn't help but smile. She had found her passion and a way to honor Grandma's legacy through the simple act of cooking.

"Thank you, Grandma," Emma whispered, tracing the faded ink of Grandma's handwriting. "You've given me more than just recipes. You've given me a path to follow."

And with that, Emma closed the recipe book, feeling grateful for the unexpected journey it had brought into her life.

Stumbled upon - Found something by chance.

- Emma stumbled upon the old recipe book in her grandmother's attic.

Culinary - Related to cooking or the kitchen.

- The thought of discovering hidden culinary secrets excited her.

Era - A period of time in history.

- Emma was transported to a different era as she flipped through the yellowed pages.

Delicate - Easily broken or damaged; fine.

- Each recipe was written in delicate cursive with notes scribbled in the margins.

Treasure - A very valuable object.

- Emma never knew she had such a treasure hidden away.

Details - Small parts that make up a whole; specifics.

- Look at the details, Emma said, tracing her finger along the handwritten notes.

Ancient - Very old.

- These recipes look ancient, Sarah remarked.

Meticulously - With great attention to detail.

- She followed the recipe meticulously, just as Grandma had written it.

Preserving - Keeping something in its original state or in good condition.

- Cooking was about preserving traditions and creating memories.

Inspired - Filled with the urge to do something.

- Inspired by her newfound passion, Emma decided to share Grandma's recipes with others.

Journey - The act of traveling from one place to another; an experience.

- People from all over the world began following her journey, trying out the recipes themselves.

Legacy - Something handed down from the past.

- Emma felt closer to Grandma and the generations of cooks who came before her through the recipes.

Unexpected - Not anticipated or predicted.

- Emma felt grateful for the unexpected journey the recipe book had brought into her life.

Passion - A strong feeling of enthusiasm or excitement for something.

- She had found her passion and a way to honor Grandma's legacy.

Flaky - Breaking easily into small thin pieces.

- The crust was flaky, and the apples were perfectly tender with just the right amount of sweetness.

18.

A DAY WITHOUT TECHNOLOGY

It was a Saturday morning like any other in the Harrison household. The sun streamed through the windows, casting a warm glow over the breakfast table where the family gathered. Mrs. Harrison, a tech-savvy entrepreneur, checked her phone for messages while Mr. Harrison scrolled through news updates on his tablet. Their teenage daughter, Lily, sat quietly in the corner with earbuds in, watching a video on her laptop.

"Hey everyone," Mr. Harrison said suddenly, breaking the electronic silence. "How about we try something different today? Let's have a day without any technology."

Mrs. Harrison looked up from her phone, eyebrows raised. "No phones, tablets, or laptops?" she asked incredulously. "Are you serious?"

Mr. Harrison nodded. "Yeah, just for one day. I think it could be good for us. We could spend more time together, maybe do something fun."

Lily took out her earbuds, curiosity piqued. "Like what, Dad?"

"Well," Mr. Harrison pondered, "we could go for a hike, play board games, cook together—anything that doesn't involve screens."

Mrs. Harrison hesitated, glancing at her phone one last time before reluctantly setting it aside. "Okay," she agreed with a sigh. "Let's give it a try."

And so, the Harrisons embarked on their day without technology. They started by packing a picnic lunch and heading to a nearby nature reserve for a hike. The air was crisp, and the sound of birds chirping filled the quiet morning. Without the distraction of notifications and emails, Mrs. Harrison found herself noticing small details—the way sunlight filtered through the trees, the scent of pine needles underfoot.

Lily, who initially protested leaving her laptop behind, soon became engrossed in the sights and sounds of nature. She pointed out a squirrel darting across the trail and stopped to admire a cluster of wildflowers blooming along the path. For the first time in a while, she felt fully present in the moment, without the constant urge to check her social media feeds.

After their hike, the Harrisons found a secluded spot by a tranquil pond to enjoy their picnic lunch. Without the distraction of screens, conversation flowed easily. They talked about their favorite hiking trails, shared funny stories from past family vacations, and debated which board game they should play later in the evening.

As the day unfolded, the family discovered new ways to connect and have fun together. They dug out old board games from the closet and spent hours laughing over competitive rounds of Monopoly. Lily, who had always been a fierce competitor, surprised everyone with her strategic moves and quick thinking.

Later in the afternoon, Mrs. Harrison suggested baking cookies together. They gathered in the kitchen, each taking on different tasks—measuring ingredients, mixing the dough, and shaping the cookies onto baking sheets. The scent of freshly baked cookies filled the air, and they eagerly waited for them to cool before devouring the warm treats.

As evening approached, the Harrisons gathered in the living

room with mugs of hot cocoa to watch a classic movie they hadn't seen in years. They snuggled under blankets, reminiscing about the first time they watched the movie together and quoting their favorite lines.

By the end of the day, the Harrisons realized how much they had enjoyed their technology-free adventure. They had connected in ways that were often overlooked in the hustle and bustle of daily life. Without the constant distractions of screens, they had rediscovered the joy of spending quality time together.

"I have to admit," Mrs. Harrison said with a smile as they prepared for bed, "today was surprisingly refreshing. I didn't realize how much I needed a break from all the technology."

Mr. Harrison nodded in agreement. "It was nice to slow down and just enjoy each other's company," he said thoughtfully. "Maybe we should do this more often."

Lily, who had put her laptop away for the day, chimed in enthusiastically. "Definitely! It was fun, and I feel like we really bonded today."

And so, as the Harrisons drifted off to sleep that night, they felt grateful for the unexpected lesson they had learned—a day without technology had brought them closer together and reminded them of the simple joys of life.

Tech-savvy - Having a good understanding of modern technology, especially computers.

- Mrs. Harrison, a tech-savvy entrepreneur, checked her phone for messages.

Incredulously - In a manner indicating disbelief.

- "No phones, tablets, or laptops?" she asked incredulously.

Curiosity - A strong desire to know or learn something.

- Lily took out her earbuds, curiosity piqued.

Pondered - Thought about something carefully before making a decision.

- "Well," Mr. Harrison pondered, "we could go for a hike, play board games, cook together—anything that doesn't involve screens."

Reluctantly - Unwillingly or hesitantly.

- Mrs. Harrison hesitated, glancing at her phone one last time before reluctantly setting it aside.

Embarked - Began a journey or project.

- And so, the Harrisons embarked on their day without technology.

Tranquil - Calm, peaceful, and quiet.

- They found a secluded spot by a tranquil pond to enjoy their picnic lunch.

Competitive - Involving a strong desire to win or be the best at something.

- They spent hours laughing over competitive rounds of Monopoly.

Strategic - Carefully planned to achieve a specific goal.

- Lily surprised everyone with her strategic moves and quick thinking.

Devouring - Eating food hungrily or quickly.

- They eagerly waited for the cookies to cool before devouring the warm treats.

Reminiscing - Recalling past experiences or events.

- They snuggled under blankets, reminiscing about the first time they watched the movie together.

Refreshing - Providing a welcome relief; pleasantly new or different.

- "Today was surprisingly refreshing," Mrs. Harrison said with a smile.

Thoughtfully - Showing careful consideration or attention.

- "It was nice to slow down and just enjoy each other's company," Mr. Harrison said thoughtfully.

Bonded - Developed a close connection or relationship with someone.

- "It was fun, and I feel like we really bonded today," Lily chimed in.

Grateful - Feeling or showing an appreciation of kindness; thankful.

- They felt grateful for the unexpected lesson they had learned.

19.

THE LOST PUPPY

It was a crisp autumn morning when Lily set out for her usual jog through the park. As she rounded a corner near the playground, she noticed a small, fluffy puppy sniffing around the base of a tree. The puppy looked lost and confused, its tail tucked between its legs.

Lily approached cautiously, not wanting to startle the timid creature. "Hey there, little one," she said softly, crouching down to the puppy's level. The puppy wagged its tail tentatively but didn't come any closer.

Lily scanned the area, hoping to spot someone who might be looking for a missing puppy. She spotted an elderly couple sitting on a bench nearby, enjoying the morning sun. "Excuse me," Lily called out politely. "Have you seen anyone looking for a puppy around here?"

The elderly woman shook her head gently. "No, dear. We've been here for a while, and we haven't seen anyone looking distressed."

Lily felt a pang of concern for the puppy. She knew she couldn't leave it alone in the park. "Do you mind if I stay with the puppy while I make a few phone calls?" she asked the couple.

"Of course, dear," the elderly man replied kindly. "Take your time."

Lily dialed the local animal shelter first, hoping they could advise her on what to do next. The receptionist sympathized with Lily's situation but explained that without a collar or microchip, they couldn't immediately take the puppy in. "Try posting on social media and local lost pet groups," the receptionist suggested. "Sometimes that's the quickest way to reunite lost pets with their owners."

Taking the receptionist's advice, Lily posted a photo of the puppy along with a brief description on social media. She included her contact information and urged anyone who recognized the puppy to reach out.

While waiting for responses, Lily sat down beside the puppy, offering it some water from her bottle. The puppy drank eagerly, its eyes darting around anxiously. "It's going to be okay," Lily reassured the puppy, gently scratching behind its ears.

Within an hour, Lily received a message from a woman named Mrs. Johnson. "I think that's our puppy, Max!" the message read. Mrs. Johnson explained that Max had slipped out of their backyard earlier that morning while she was busy with chores.

Lily arranged to meet Mrs. Johnson at the park entrance. As they approached each other, Max's tail started wagging furiously. He recognized Mrs. Johnson's voice and scent from a distance. Lily smiled as she handed Max over to his relieved owner.

"Thank you so much," Mrs. Johnson said gratefully, tears welling up in her eyes. "I don't know what I would have done if you hadn't found him."

Lily shrugged off the praise. "I'm just glad I could help," she replied modestly.

As Mrs. Johnson walked away, cradling Max in her arms, Lily couldn't help but feel a sense of satisfaction. Helping reunite a lost puppy with its owner had been a heartwarming experience—one that reaffirmed her belief in the kindness of strangers and the importance of lending a helping hand when needed.

As she resumed her jog through the park, Lily couldn't help but smile at the memory of Max's wagging tail and Mrs. Johnson's tearful gratitude. Sometimes, she thought, the smallest acts of kindness could make the biggest difference in someone's day.

Cautiously - In a way that avoids potential problems or dangers.

- Lily approached cautiously, not wanting to startle the timid creature.

Timid - Showing a lack of courage or confidence; easily frightened.

- The puppy looked lost and confused, its tail tucked between its legs.

Concern - A feeling of worry, especially about something important.

- Lily felt a pang of concern for the puppy.

Advise - To offer suggestions about the best course of action to someone.

- The receptionist sympathized with Lily's situation but explained that without a collar or microchip, they couldn't immediately take the puppy in.

Sympathized - Felt or expressed compassion for someone.

- The receptionist sympathized with Lily's situation but explained that without a collar or microchip, they couldn't immediately take the puppy in.

Reunite - To bring together again after being separated.

- Try posting on social media and local lost pet groups; sometimes that's the quickest way to reunite lost pets with their owners.

Anxiously - In a manner resulting from or revealing anxiety.

- The puppy drank eagerly, its eyes darting around anxiously.

Relieved - No longer feeling distressed or anxious; reassured.

- Lily smiled as she handed Max over to his relieved owner.

Gratefully - With appreciation for something done or received.

- "Thank you so much," Mrs. Johnson said gratefully, tears welling up in her eyes.

Modestly - In an unassuming manner, without bragging or boasting.

- "I'm just glad I could help," she replied modestly.

Affirmed - Confirmed or ratified something as true.

- Helping reunite a lost puppy with its owner had been a heartwarming experience—one that reaffirmed her belief in the kindness of strangers.

Gratitude - The quality of being thankful; readiness to show appreciation.

- Lily couldn't help but smile at the memory of Max's wagging tail and Mrs. Johnson's tearful gratitude.

Cradling - Holding gently and protectively.

- Mrs. Johnson walked away, cradling Max in her arms.

20.

THE MUSIC BOX

Emily loved exploring her grandmother's attic. It was a treasure trove of forgotten relics from decades past—old photographs in sepia tones, dusty books with yellowed pages, and trinkets that whispered tales of times gone by. But there was one item that always intrigued Emily the most: a small, intricately carved music box tucked away in a corner.

The music box had been in the family for generations. Emily's grandmother often spoke fondly of it, recounting how her own grandmother had received it as a gift from a mysterious traveler who passed through their village long ago. The box played a hauntingly beautiful melody that seemed to transport listeners to another era.

One lazy summer afternoon, Emily decided to delve deeper into the mysteries of the music box. She carefully lifted it from its resting place and cradled it in her hands. The wood was smooth and polished, with delicate carvings of roses and vines adorning its surface. Gently winding the key, Emily held her breath as the lid opened with a soft click, revealing the intricate mechanism inside.

As the music box began to play, Emily closed her eyes and let the melody wash over her. It was as if time itself had paused, allowing her to immerse herself in the music and imagine the stories it held within.

Lost in the enchanting melody, Emily began to wonder about the secrets the music box might hold. What journeys had it been on? Whose hands had turned its key over the years?

And most importantly, what memories and stories had it witnessed?

Suddenly, a piece of paper fluttered out from between the folds of fabric inside the music box. Emily's heart skipped a beat as she carefully unfolded it. The paper was yellowed with age, its edges frayed, but the words written in elegant script were still legible.

"To my dearest Margaret," the note began. "May this music box always remind you of our summer days by the lake, where we laughed and dreamed of a future filled with love and adventure."

Emily's curiosity peaked. Who was Margaret? And who had written this heartfelt message? She gently placed the note aside and continued exploring the contents of the music box.

Amidst the velvet-lined interior, Emily discovered a small, faded photograph. It depicted a young woman with soft curls framing her face, holding hands with a dashing young man beside a sunlit lake. They were smiling, their eyes sparkling with joy and promise.

Emily realized that this must be Margaret and her beloved. The photograph captured a moment frozen in time, a snapshot of a love story that had endured through the ages.

As the music box continued to play its haunting melody, Emily felt a sense of connection to Margaret and her story. She imagined the summer days spent by the lake, the laughter echoing across the water, and the dreams shared under the shade of ancient trees.

With a renewed sense of wonder, Emily decided to share her discovery with her grandmother. Together, they sat in the attic, reminiscing about the past and weaving tales around the music box and its enchanting melody. They speculated about the lives of Margaret and her beloved, imagining the adventures they must have embarked upon together.

Emily's grandmother smiled warmly, her eyes reflecting a lifetime of memories. "The music box holds more than just a melody," she mused. "It holds the stories of those who came before us, their dreams, their hopes, and their love."

And so, Emily's afternoon in the attic turned into an exploration of family history and a celebration of the enduring power of music and love. The old music box had revealed its secrets, connecting Emily to her ancestors and leaving her with a deeper appreciation for the mysteries hidden within everyday treasures.

Intrigued - Interested and curious.

- Emily was intrigued by the small, intricately carved music box tucked away in a corner.

Generations - All of the people born and living at about the same time, regarded collectively.

- The music box had been in the family for generations.

Mysterious - Difficult or impossible to understand, explain, or identify.

- Emily's grandmother received the music box as a gift from a mysterious traveler.

Hauntingly - In a way that is poignant and evocative.

- The box played a hauntingly beautiful melody that seemed to transport listeners to another era.

Enchanted - Filled with delight; charmed.

- Lost in the enchanting melody, Emily began to wonder about the secrets the music box might hold.

Curiosity - A strong desire to know or learn something.

- Emily's curiosity peaked when she found a piece of paper inside the music box.

Heartfelt - Sincere and deeply felt.

- Who had written this heartfelt message?

Depicted - Represented or shown in a particular form.

- The photograph depicted a young woman with soft curls framing her face.

Endured - Suffered something painful or difficult patiently.

- The photograph captured a love story that had endured through the ages.

Connection - A relationship in which a person, thing, or idea is linked or associated with something else.

- Emily felt a sense of connection to Margaret and her story.

Reminiscing - Indulging in enjoyable recollection of past events.

- Together, they sat in the attic, reminiscing about the past.

Speculated - Formed a theory or conjecture about a subject without firm evidence.

- They speculated about the lives of Margaret and her beloved.

Enduring - Continuing or long-lasting.

- Emily's afternoon in the attic turned into a celebration of the enduring power of music and love.

Revealed - Made known through divine inspiration.

- The old music box had revealed its secrets, connecting Emily to her ancestors.

21.

THE DREAM JOB

Sarah had always dreamed of working in a bustling office, surrounded by colleagues who shared her passion for marketing. Armed with a degree in Business Administration, she embarked on the daunting journey of job hunting, determined to find her place in the corporate world.

After countless applications and nerve-wracking interviews, Sarah finally received the call she had been eagerly awaiting. "Congratulations, Sarah! We're pleased to offer you the position of Marketing Assistant at Bright Horizons Advertising," said Mr. Thompson, the HR manager.

Sarah couldn't believe her luck. Bright Horizons was known for its innovative campaigns and vibrant workplace culture. It was the perfect opportunity to kick-start her career in marketing. With a mix of excitement and nervousness, she accepted the offer and prepared herself for the challenges ahead.

On her first day at Bright Horizons, Sarah was greeted by friendly faces and the bustling energy of the office. Her desk was adorned with a welcome bouquet and a stack of onboarding documents. She took a moment to soak in the atmosphere, feeling a surge of pride and determination.

Throughout her first week, Sarah dove headfirst into her responsibilities. She assisted the senior marketers with market research, brainstormed creative ideas for upcoming campaigns, and learned the ins and outs of the company's digital platforms. Each day presented new opportunities to learn and grow.

However, amidst the excitement of her dream job, Sarah soon encountered the realities of office politics. She noticed subtle tensions between teams, disagreements over project priorities, and occasional clashes of egos during meetings. It was a side of corporate life she hadn't anticipated during her college years.

One particular project, the launch of a new product line for a client, tested Sarah's patience and diplomatic skills. As the Marketing Assistant, she was tasked with coordinating between the creative team, the client's representatives, and the senior management at Bright Horizons. The pressure was immense, but Sarah was determined to prove herself.

During a crucial brainstorming session, Sarah found herself caught in the crossfire of differing opinions. The creative team wanted to push boundaries with a bold campaign, while the client preferred a more conservative approach. Sarah listened attentively to both sides, carefully weighing the pros and cons of each approach.

In the midst of heated discussions, Sarah remembered the advice of her mentor from college: "In any job, especially in marketing, it's crucial to navigate office politics with grace and professionalism. Remember, everyone has the same goal—to deliver exceptional results for the client."

With this wisdom in mind, Sarah took a step back and proposed a compromise that incorporated elements from both perspectives. To her relief, the room fell silent as her suggestion was met with thoughtful nods and agreements. It was a small victory that boosted Sarah's confidence and earned her respect among her colleagues.

As the launch date approached, Sarah worked tirelessly alongside her team to bring the campaign to life. Late nights turned into early mornings, filled with last-minute adjustments and final tweaks to ensure everything was perfect. The experience taught Sarah the value of perseverance and collaboration in achieving success.

On the day of the product launch, Sarah stood proudly among her colleagues as they unveiled the campaign to the client and the media. The feedback was overwhelmingly positive, with praises for the innovative approach and strategic execution. Sarah felt a deep sense of satisfaction knowing that her hard work had paid off.

Reflecting on her journey to her dream job, Sarah realized that while office politics could be challenging, they were also opportunities for growth and learning. Each interaction, whether smooth or fraught with tension, taught her valuable lessons in communication, negotiation, and resilience.

As Sarah settled into her role at Bright Horizons, she remained grateful for the support of her colleagues and mentors who believed in her abilities. With each passing day, she continued to thrive in her career, fueled by her passion for marketing and the drive to make a meaningful impact in the industry.

Embarked - To start or undertake a journey, activity, or venture.

- Armed with a degree in Business Administration, Sarah embarked on the daunting journey of job hunting.

Innovative - Introducing or using new ideas, methods, or concepts.

- Bright Horizons was known for its innovative campaigns and vibrant workplace culture.

Diplomatic - Having or showing an ability to deal with people in a sensitive and tactful way.

- Sarah's diplomatic skills were tested during the project launch when handling disagreements between the creative team and the client.

Navigate - To find one's way or manage a situation, especially with skill.

- Sarah navigated office politics with grace and professionalism, ensuring smooth collaboration on the project.

Compromise - An agreement or settlement of a dispute that is reached by each side making concessions.

- Sarah proposed a compromise that satisfied both the creative team's desire for innovation and the client's preference for conservatism.

Perseverance - Persistence in doing something despite difficulty or delay in achieving success.

- The late nights and early mornings demonstrated Sarah's perseverance in ensuring the campaign's success.

Resilience - The capacity to recover quickly from difficulties; toughness.

- Sarah's resilience was evident as she faced challenges during the project launch but continued to work diligently towards achieving the goals.

Collaboration - The action of working with someone to produce or create something.

- Sarah learned the value of collaboration while working alongside her team to bring the campaign to life.

Interaction - Communication or direct involvement with someone or something.

- Each interaction with colleagues and clients provided Sarah with opportunities to learn and grow in her career.

Feedback - Information about reactions to a product, a person's performance of a task, etc., used as a basis for improvement.

- The overwhelmingly positive feedback from the client and media boosted Sarah's confidence in her abilities.

22.

THE KINDNESS CHALLENGE

At Jefferson High School, the start of each school year brought with it new challenges and opportunities for students and staff alike. This year, however, Principal Thompson had something special in mind to kick-start positivity and unity among the students: The Kindness Challenge.

It all began during the first assembly of the semester. Principal Thompson stood tall on the stage, his voice projecting warmth and enthusiasm through the gymnasium. "Good morning, students! I hope you've all had a wonderful summer break," he began, eliciting cheers and laughter from the crowd.

"As we embark on another school year, I want to introduce something that will not only make our school a better place but will also leave a lasting impact on each of you," Principal Thompson continued. He paused, allowing the anticipation to build before revealing the details of The Kindness Challenge.

"The Kindness Challenge is simple yet powerful," Principal Thompson explained. "For the next month, I challenge each and every one of you to perform acts of kindness—big or small—towards your fellow classmates, teachers, and even strangers in the community."

The students exchanged curious glances, some nodding in agreement while others whispered excitedly to their friends. The idea of spreading kindness resonated deeply with many, including Emily, a senior known for her academic prowess and leadership qualities.

As the assembly concluded, Emily found herself approached by her close friends, Sarah and Alex. "What do you think about The Kindness Challenge?" Sarah asked, adjusting her backpack strap over her shoulder.

"I think it's a fantastic initiative," Emily replied with a smile. "Imagine the impact we could make just by being a little kinder to each other. I'm in!"

And so, The Kindness Challenge began. Throughout the halls of Jefferson High School, students embraced the spirit of the challenge with enthusiasm. Small gestures like holding doors open, complimenting each other's outfits, and sharing study tips became commonplace. It was heartwarming to see students from different cliques and backgrounds coming together in acts of kindness.

One particularly memorable moment occurred during lunchtime in the cafeteria. Emily noticed a freshman, Lily, sitting alone at a table, quietly eating her sandwich. Lily was new to the school and often seemed shy around her peers.

Emily approached Lily with a warm smile. "Hey, Lily! Mind if I join you for lunch?" she asked, pulling out a chair opposite her.

Lily looked up, surprised but grateful. "Um, sure. I mean, yeah, that would be nice," she replied, nervously adjusting her glasses.

As they chatted over lunch, Emily learned that Lily was passionate about photography and loved reading mystery novels. Emily shared her own interests in science and mentioned the upcoming science fair that Lily might be interested in joining.

By the end of lunch, Lily seemed more at ease, her smile brighter than before. Emily felt a sense of fulfillment knowing that a simple act of kindness had made a difference in someone's day.

Outside of school, The Kindness Challenge continued to inspire positive change. Students volunteered at local charities, organized fundraisers for community causes, and even started a school-wide recycling program to reduce waste.

However, the true impact of The Kindness Challenge extended beyond tangible acts. It fostered a culture of empathy, compassion, and inclusivity among the students. Friendships blossomed, stereotypes were shattered, and a sense of unity flourished within the school community.

As the month drew to a close, Principal Thompson gathered the students once again for a final assembly to celebrate the success of The Kindness Challenge. "I am incredibly proud of each and every one of you," he began, his voice filled with genuine admiration.

"Throughout this challenge, you've demonstrated the power of kindness in creating a positive school environment. Whether it was offering a helping hand, lending an ear, or simply sharing a smile, your actions have made a profound difference," Principal Thompson continued, prompting applause and cheers from the students.

Emily, Sarah, and Alex exchanged proud glances, knowing they had been part of something truly special. The Kindness Challenge had not only transformed their school but had also left an indelible mark on their hearts.

As the school year progressed, the spirit of kindness persisted. Students carried forward the lessons learned from The Kindness Challenge, making kindness a habit rather than a one-time event. It was a reminder that even small acts of kindness could ignite positive change and create a more compassionate world.

Enthusiasm - Intense and eager enjoyment, interest, or approval.

- Principal Thompson's enthusiasm for The Kindness Challenge was evident as he addressed the students in the assembly.

Initiative - The ability to assess and initiate things independently; enterprise.

- Emily showed initiative by organizing study groups as part of The Kindness Challenge to help her classmates prepare for exams.

Prowess - Skill or expertise in a particular activity or field.

- Emily was known for her academic prowess, which earned her respect among her peers and teachers.

Heartwarming - Causing feelings of warmth and pleasure.

- It was heartwarming to see students from different backgrounds coming together to participate in The Kindness Challenge.

Cliques - A small group of people, with shared interests or other features in common, who spend time together and do not readily allow others to join them.

- The Kindness Challenge encouraged students to break out of their cliques and interact with peers they wouldn't normally engage with.

Compassion - Sympathetic pity and concern for the sufferings or misfortunes of others.

- The Kindness Challenge fostered a culture of compassion as students reached out to support each other during challenging times.

Empathy - The ability to understand and share the feelings of another.

- Through The Kindness Challenge, students developed empathy by putting themselves in the shoes of their peers and showing understanding.

Inclusivity - The practice or policy of including people who might otherwise be excluded or marginalized.

- The Kindness Challenge promoted inclusivity by encouraging all students to participate regardless of their background or social status.

Indelible - Not able to be forgotten or removed.

- The Kindness Challenge left an indelible mark on the school community, creating lasting memories and positive change.

Persistence - Firm or obstinate continuance in a course of action in spite of difficulty or opposition.

- The students' persistence in practicing kindness, even after The Kindness Challenge ended, helped to sustain a positive school environment.

23.

THE MYSTERY OF THE OLD LIBRARY

It was a hot summer afternoon when Emma and Jake, siblings aged 12 and 10 respectively, found themselves at their town's old library. With school out for vacation, their mom had decided it was the perfect time for them to explore the library and cultivate their love for books.

As they entered the library, a cool breeze greeted them, a refreshing change from the scorching sun outside. The library was a haven of quietude, with rows upon rows of bookshelves stretching from the polished wooden floors to the high ceiling. The air was tinged with the scent of old paper and dust, creating an atmosphere of mystery and nostalgia.

"Wow, Emma, look at all these books!" Jake exclaimed, his eyes wide with wonder as he scanned the shelves filled with books of various sizes and colors.

Emma smiled, her excitement matching her brother's. "I know, Jake! This place is amazing. Let's start with the children's section and then explore the rest of the library," she suggested, leading the way towards a corner where colorful picture books beckoned.

After spending some time browsing through the children's section and selecting a few books to borrow, Emma and Jake decided to venture deeper into the library. They passed through aisles of history books, biographies, and fiction novels until they reached a section marked "Rare Books and Archives."

Curiosity piqued, Emma scanned the titles of the ancient-looking books lining the shelves. "Look at these, Jake. These books must be really old," she remarked, gently running her fingers over the faded leather covers.

Jake nodded enthusiastically. "Do you think there are any secrets hidden in these books, Emma? Like treasure maps or messages from pirates?"

Emma chuckled. "I don't know about treasure maps, but old books can hold all sorts of secrets. Let's keep our eyes open."

As they moved further into the archives section, Emma noticed something peculiar—a section of the wall near the end of the aisle seemed slightly different from the rest. "Jake, come here! Look at this wall," she whispered, her curiosity now fully ignited.

Jake hurried over, his eyes narrowing as he examined the wall closely. "It does look different, Emma. It's like there's a seam running along here," he observed, tracing his finger along the seemingly seamless edge.

With a shared look of excitement, Emma and Jake pushed against the wall, and to their amazement, it swung open noiselessly, revealing a narrow passageway hidden behind. They exchanged wide-eyed glances before stepping cautiously into the darkness, their hearts pounding with anticipation.

The passageway led them into a small, dimly lit room. Emma flicked on a light switch, revealing shelves filled with dusty old books, ancient manuscripts, and artifacts that seemed to tell stories of bygone eras. In the center of the room stood an ornate wooden desk covered with yellowed parchment and quill pens.

"Whoa, Emma! We found a hidden room in the library!" Jake exclaimed, his voice echoing softly in the confined space.

Emma grinned, her excitement palpable. "This is incredible, Jake. Imagine the history hidden in these books and documents. I wonder why it was kept secret."

As they explored further, Jake stumbled upon a leather-bound journal tucked away in a corner of the room. "Emma, look at this journal! It seems really old," he exclaimed, carefully opening its fragile pages.

Together, they read passages written in elegant cursive handwriting, detailing the daily life of a librarian from decades past. The journal spoke of the library's rich history, the people who frequented it, and even hinted at hidden treasures rumored to be buried beneath the library's foundations.

Hours passed as Emma and Jake immersed themselves in the mysteries of the old library room. They made notes, took photographs of significant artifacts, and even found a hidden compartment in the desk containing old photographs of the town dating back to the early 1900s.

Eventually, the sun began to set, casting long shadows through the small window of the hidden room. Reluctantly, Emma and Jake decided it was time to leave, but they promised each other they would return to unravel more mysteries of the old library.

As they emerged from the hidden passageway back into the main library, they found themselves greeted by the librarian, Ms. Thompson, who looked both surprised and amused. "Well, well, what have we here?" she asked, her eyes twinkling with curiosity as she glanced at the dust on their clothes.

Emma and Jake exchanged a knowing smile. "We found something amazing, Ms. Thompson. A hidden room in the library!" Emma exclaimed, unable to contain her excitement.

Ms. Thompson's eyebrows shot up in surprise. "A hidden room, you say? Well, it seems the library still has its secrets," she mused, leading them back towards the entrance.

As they bid farewell to Ms. Thompson and stepped out into the warm evening air, Emma and Jake couldn't stop talking about their adventure. They knew that the discovery of the hidden room in the old library would be a story they would cherish and share for years to come.

And so, with hearts full of wonder and curiosity, Emma and Jake looked forward to their next visit to the library, eager to uncover more secrets and unravel the mysteries of the past.

Curiosity - A strong desire to know or learn something.

- Jake's curiosity about the hidden room in the library led him and Emma to discover its secrets.

Peculiar - Strange or unusual, especially in a way that is interesting or suspicious.

- Emma noticed a peculiar seam along the wall of the archives section, sparking their investigation.

Anticipation - The feeling of excited expectation about something that is going to happen.

- As they entered the hidden passageway, Emma and Jake's hearts pounded with anticipation of what they might find.

Ornate - Elaborately decorated; very detailed and complex.

- The wooden desk in the hidden room was adorned with ornate carvings and delicate inlays.

Elegant - Graceful and stylish in appearance or manner.

- The journal they found in the hidden room was written in elegant cursive handwriting, detailing historical anecdotes.

Fragile - Easily broken or damaged, delicate.

- Jake handled the leather-bound journal with care, aware of its fragile condition due to age.

Immense - Extremely large or great, especially in scale or degree.

- Emma felt immense excitement as they uncovered artifacts and old documents in the hidden room.

Palpable - Able to be touched or felt; tangible.

- The excitement in the air was palpable as Emma and Jake explored the mysteries of the old library room.

Reluctantly - With hesitation, unwillingly.

- Reluctantly, Emma and Jake decided it was time to leave the hidden room as the sun began to set.

Twinkling - Shining with a flickering or sparkling light.

- Ms. Thompson's eyes twinkled with curiosity when she heard about Emma and Jake's discovery of the hidden room.

24.

THE MARATHON RUNNER

In the heart of Willowvale, a quaint town nestled between rolling hills and lush green forests, lived a man named David who had always been fascinated by the idea of running a marathon. David was not a professional athlete; in fact, he worked a nine-to-five job at the local bookstore, where he spent his days surrounded by shelves of books that sparked his imagination.

One rainy afternoon, as David flipped through a magazine during his lunch break, he stumbled upon an article about marathon running. The stories of ordinary people pushing their limits and achieving extraordinary feats stirred something deep within him. With a mixture of excitement and determination, David decided that he would run a marathon—a daunting 26.2-mile journey that would test his endurance and perseverance.

David knew that preparing for a marathon would require dedication and hard work. He began by researching training plans and gradually increasing his running mileage. His mornings now started with brisk runs through Willowvale's peaceful streets, where the cool morning air filled his lungs and energized his spirit.

As the weeks turned into months, David's passion for running grew stronger. He embraced the challenge of pushing his body further than ever before, learning to pace himself and build stamina. Along the way, he encountered setbacks—aching muscles, blisters on his feet, and days when the weather seemed determined to thwart his training efforts. Yet, with each hurdle, David remained steadfast in his goal, drawing strength from the support of his friends and the encouraging words of his coach, Sarah, a fellow runner who had completed several marathons herself.

"It's all about consistency and listening to your body," Sarah would remind David during their weekly training sessions at the town's outdoor track. "You've got this, David. Believe in yourself."

One chilly morning, David embarked on his longest training run yet—a grueling 20-mile trek through Willowvale's scenic countryside. The sun rose slowly over the horizon, casting a golden glow on the frost-kissed fields and sparkling streams. With each step, David felt a sense of exhilaration and anticipation building within him. He knew that this run would be a pivotal moment in his marathon journey.

As David navigated winding trails and conquered steep inclines, he reflected on the lessons he had learned along the way. Perseverance, he realized, was not just about physical endurance but also about mental resilience. There were moments when doubt crept in, tempting him to give up, but David pushed through, focusing on the finish line that awaited him.

The support of the Willowvale community also played a crucial role in David's journey. During his training runs, neighbors would wave and cheer him on from their porches, offering words of encouragement and a sense of camaraderie that fueled his determination. Their belief in him strengthened his resolve to cross the marathon's finish line.

Finally, race day arrived—a crisp autumn morning tinged with excitement and nervous energy. David stood among thousands of other runners at the starting line, the rhythmic beat of his heart matching the pulse of the crowd. As the starting gun echoed through the air, he set off with a surge of adrenaline, his eyes fixed on the road ahead.

The marathon course wound through Willowvale's picturesque landscapes, past towering oak trees and quaint farmhouses adorned with festive banners. Spectators lined the streets, holding colorful signs and cheering enthusiastically for the runners. David soaked in the energy of the crowd, drawing strength from their cheers as he tackled each mile with determination.

Throughout the race, David faced moments of exhaustion and doubt. His legs felt heavy, and his body screamed for rest, but he refused to give in. He reminded himself of the countless early mornings and long training runs that had led him to this moment. With each stride, he pushed forward, visualizing the finish line growing closer with every step.

As David approached the final stretch of the marathon, emotions swelled within him—a mixture of fatigue, triumph, and overwhelming joy. The cheers of the crowd echoed in his ears, urging him onward. With a final burst of energy, he sprinted across the finish line, arms raised triumphantly above his head.

Tears welled up in David's eyes as he received a finisher's medal, a tangible symbol of his perseverance and determination. Amidst the post-race celebrations, he embraced Sarah and thanked her for her unwavering support throughout his marathon journey.

"You did it, David," Sarah exclaimed, her eyes shining with pride. "I knew you had it in you."

In the days that followed, David reflected on his marathon experience—a journey that had tested his limits, strengthened his resolve, and taught him the true meaning of perseverance.

The lessons he learned on the roads of Willowvale would stay with him for a lifetime, inspiring him to tackle new challenges with courage and determination.

As David returned to his job at the bookstore, he found himself sharing his marathon story with customers and colleagues alike. His journey had not only transformed him physically but had also ignited a passion for running and a belief in the power of setting ambitious goals.

In the heart of Willowvale, where the hills whispered tales of triumph and the streets echoed with the footsteps of runners, David's journey stood as a testament to the human spirit's ability to persevere and achieve greatness. His story inspired others in the community to lace up their running shoes and chase their own dreams, one step at a time.

Determination - Firmness of purpose; the quality of being resolute.

- David's determination to complete the marathon never wavered, despite the challenges he faced along the way.

Endurance - The ability to sustain prolonged physical or mental effort.

- Training for a marathon requires building endurance through long-distance running and strength training.

Resilience - The capacity to recover quickly from difficulties; toughness.

- David's mental resilience helped him push through moments of doubt during the marathon.

Stamina - The ability to sustain prolonged physical or mental effort; endurance.

- Building stamina through regular exercise and proper

nutrition is essential for marathon runners.

Triumph - A great victory or achievement.

- Crossing the marathon finish line was a moment of triumph for David after months of training.

Exhilaration - A feeling of excitement, happiness, or elation.

- David felt a sense of exhilaration as he completed his longest training run through the countryside.

Camaraderie - Mutual trust and friendship among people who spend a lot of time together.

- The camaraderie among runners during the marathon created a supportive atmosphere.

Adrenaline - A hormone released in response to stress or excitement, increasing alertness and physical readiness.

- David felt a surge of adrenaline as he heard the starting gun for the marathon race.

Resolve - Firm determination to do something.

- With unwavering resolve, David pushed through the final miles of the marathon.

Embrace - To accept or support willingly and enthusiastically.

- David embraced the challenge of running a marathon with enthusiasm and dedication.

25.

A FAREWELL TO REMEMBER

In the quaint town of Riverdale, nestled amidst rolling hills and blooming orchards, lived a community bound together by warmth and camaraderie. Each year, they gathered for the Harvest Festival—a jubilant celebration of abundance and togetherness.

Among the townsfolk was Emma, a spirited young woman with a passion for painting. Her vibrant canvases captured the essence of Riverdale—the emerald meadows, the shimmering river, and the cozy cottages nestled under canopies of ancient oaks. Her art adorned the walls of local galleries and stirred the hearts of those who beheld it.

As summer drew to a close, whispers of change rustled through Riverdale. Emma's father had received a job offer in a distant city—a promising opportunity that would provide for their family's future. Although excited for the prospects ahead, Emma grappled with a bittersweet truth—she would soon bid farewell to the only home she had ever known.

On the eve of the Harvest Festival, a melancholy haze settled over Emma as she gazed out at the sunset-drenched landscape from her bedroom window. The soft hues of amber and rose painted the sky, mirroring the conflicting emotions swirling in her heart.

Downstairs, the aroma of freshly baked apple pie filled the air —a cherished family recipe passed down through generations.

Emma's mother hummed a familiar tune as she rolled out dough, her smile tinged with a hint of nostalgia. "The festival will be a wonderful send-off, dear," she said, her voice gentle yet laden with unspoken sentiment.

The next morning, Emma donned her favorite sweater—a cozy knit adorned with splashes of color reminiscent of her paintings. She joined the bustling procession making its way to the town square, where the Harvest Festival awaited in all its glory.

Stalls brimmed with ripe fruits, artisanal crafts, and savory treats that tantalized the senses. Laughter echoed through the air as children chased each other through fields adorned with ribbons and wreaths. Musicians serenaded the crowd with melodies that seemed to dance upon the breeze.

Amidst the festivities, Emma found herself drawn to a familiar oak tree—the same tree where she had spent countless afternoons sketching and daydreaming. Its sturdy trunk offered solace amidst the whirlwind of farewells and new beginnings.

As she traced her fingers along the bark, lost in memories of seasons past, a voice called out her name. Emma turned to find Mr. Thompson, the town's elder and keeper of its history, approaching with a gentle smile.

"Emma," he began, his voice rich with wisdom and affection, "I've watched you grow from a curious child into a remarkable artist who captures the very essence of our beloved Riverdale."

Emma's cheeks flushed with warmth at his words. Mr. Thompson continued, his gaze soft yet steadfast. "Change is the heartbeat of life, my dear. As you embark on this new chapter, remember that your roots here will always be a part of who you are."

His words resonated deeply within Emma's heart. She nodded,

her eyes glistening with unshed tears, and thanked him for his kindness and wisdom. Mr. Thompson clasped her hand in his weathered one—a gesture of reassurance and solidarity.

As dusk descended upon Riverdale, the festival culminated in a grand bonfire—a beacon of warmth and unity amidst the encroaching darkness. Townsfolk gathered around its flickering glow, sharing stories and songs that echoed through the night.

Emma stood among them, her heart overflowing with gratitude for the community that had shaped her into the person she had become. She joined hands with friends and neighbors, weaving through the dance of laughter and whispered wishes for the future.

At the bonfire's peak, Emma stepped forward, her voice steady yet infused with emotion. "To Riverdale," she declared, her words carrying across the gathering like a gentle breeze, "where memories bloom and hearts forever find a home."

In that moment, under the starlit sky and amidst the flickering embers, Emma knew that farewells were not endings but beginnings—a testament to the enduring bonds of love, belonging, and the timeless spirit of Riverdale.

And as the last notes of laughter faded into the night, Emma carried with her the promise of new horizons, knowing that wherever life's journey led, the spirit of Riverdale would forever dwell within her.

Melancholy - A feeling of pensive sadness, typically with no obvious cause.

- On the eve of her departure, Emma was overwhelmed by a sense of melancholy as she looked out over the familiar landscape of Riverdale.

Solace - Comfort or consolation in a time of distress or sadness.

- The familiar oak tree provided Emma with solace as she grappled with the impending farewell to her beloved town.

Affection - A gentle feeling of fondness or liking.

- Mr. Thompson spoke with affection as he praised Emma's growth as an artist and shared wisdom about embracing change.

Reassurance - The action of removing someone's doubts or fears.

- Mr. Thompson's gesture of clasping Emma's hand was a gesture of reassurance, conveying his support and understanding.

Culminated - Reached its highest point or climax.

- The Harvest Festival culminated in a grand bonfire, marking the peak of celebrations and unity in Riverdale.

Enduring - Continuing or long-lasting.

- Emma carried with her the enduring bonds of love and belonging that she had experienced in Riverdale.

Horizons - The limits of one's knowledge, experience, or interest.

- Emma looked forward to new horizons as she embarked on her journey beyond Riverdale, eager to explore new opportunities.

Unity - The state of being united or joined as a whole.

- The bonfire symbolized unity as townsfolk gathered together, sharing stories and songs under the starlit sky.

Encroaching - Gradually advancing beyond usual or

acceptable limits.

- The encroaching darkness of night contrasted with the warmth and light of the festival's bonfire.

Resonated - Evoke or suggest images, memories, and emotions.

- Mr. Thompson's words resonated deeply with Emma, reminding her of the importance of embracing change while cherishing her roots.

26.

THE LAST TRAIN HOME

It was a crisp autumn evening in the bustling city of Brookton. Sarah, a young traveler with a penchant for adventure, found herself exploring the vibrant streets lined with shops, cafes, and neon-lit signs. She had spent the day wandering through museums and art galleries, immersing herself in the city's rich culture and history.

As the sun dipped below the horizon, Sarah realized it was time to head back to her hostel. Consulting her watch, she hurried towards the metro station, eager to catch the last train home. The metro was a lifeline in Brookton, crisscrossing the city and connecting its diverse neighborhoods.

Arriving at the station, Sarah was greeted by the familiar sound of trains rumbling in and out. She checked the electronic board for departure times, only to find that the last train to her neighborhood had departed just minutes ago. Disappointment washed over her as she realized she would have to wait until morning for the next train.

Not wanting to waste time, Sarah decided to make the most of her unexpected predicament. She ventured outside the station and wandered through the streets, curious about what the city had to offer after dark. Neon lights cast a soft glow over the sidewalks, and the air was filled with the aroma of street food and laughter from late-night revelers.

Sarah stumbled upon a quaint alleyway adorned with colorful

murals—a hidden gem that she might have missed if she had caught the train on time. Intrigued, she wandered down the alley, snapping photos of the artwork that depicted scenes from Brookton's history and culture.

As she walked, Sarah noticed a small, cozy cafe tucked away in a corner. The warm glow of the lights and the inviting aroma of freshly brewed coffee drew her in. Inside, she found herself surrounded by locals engaged in lively conversations, savoring pastries and sharing stories over steaming cups of espresso.

Sarah struck up a conversation with the barista, who recommended a local specialty—a flaky pastry filled with cream and topped with powdered sugar. Delighted by the unexpected culinary delight, Sarah savored each bite, appreciating the flavors and the hospitality of the cafe.

Feeling refreshed and energized, Sarah continued her exploration of the city's hidden corners. She stumbled upon a small bookstore with shelves lined with books in different languages and genres. The bookseller, an elderly gentleman with a twinkle in his eye, shared stories of the neighborhood's history and recommended a classic novel set in Brookton.

Sarah spent hours browsing through the bookstore, losing herself in the pages of a gripping mystery novel set against the backdrop of the city she had come to love. Time seemed to stand still as she immersed herself in the world of the characters, their adventures unfolding in parallel to her own unexpected journey through Brookton's nighttime streets.

Eventually, the sky began to lighten, signaling the approach of dawn. Sarah realized it was time to make her way back to the metro station, where she would catch the first train home. As she walked through the quiet streets, she reflected on the night's events—the chance encounter with the cafe, the serendipitous discovery of the bookstore, and the warmth of the people she had met along the way.

Boarding the train, Sarah felt a sense of gratitude for the unexpected detour that had allowed her to see a different side of Brookton. She knew that she would cherish the memories of this night for years to come—a reminder of the beauty and magic that could be found in the most unexpected places.

As the train rattled towards her neighborhood, Sarah smiled to herself, eager to share her adventure with friends and family. She had missed the last train home, but in doing so, she had found something far more valuable—a hidden part of the city and a treasure trove of experiences that had enriched her journey in ways she could never have imagined.

Quaint - Attractively unusual or old-fashioned.

- Sarah stumbled upon a quaint alleyway adorned with colorful murals, a hidden gem in the bustling city.

Predicament - A difficult, unpleasant, or embarrassing situation.

- Missing the last train home left Sarah in an unexpected predicament, forcing her to explore Brookton's nighttime streets.

Aroma - A distinctive, typically pleasant smell.

- Inside the cozy cafe, Sarah was greeted by the inviting aroma of freshly brewed coffee and pastries.

Hospitality - The friendly and generous reception and entertainment of guests, visitors, or strangers.

- Sarah appreciated the hospitality of the locals at the cafe, who engaged her in lively conversations.

Serendipitous - Occurring or discovered by chance in a happy or beneficial way.

- Sarah's discovery of the small bookstore was serendipitous, leading her to spend hours immersed in a gripping novel.

Detour - A long or roundabout route taken to avoid something or to visit somewhere along the way.

- Missing her train home turned into a delightful detour through the hidden corners of Brookton.

Cherish - To protect and care for (someone) lovingly.

- Sarah cherished the memories of her unexpected adventure in Brookton, knowing they would stay with her for years to come.

Serene - Calm, peaceful, and untroubled; tranquil.

- Sarah found herself walking through the quiet streets of Brookton at dawn, enjoying the serene atmosphere before catching her train.

Immerse - To involve oneself deeply in a particular activity or interest.

- Sarah immersed herself in the world of the characters in the novel, losing track of time as she read.

Enrich - To improve or enhance the quality or value of something.

- Sarah's journey through Brookton's hidden places enriched her understanding and appreciation of the city's culture and history.

27.

THE CHARITY EVENT

The bustling town of Willowbrook was abuzz with excitement and anticipation as the sun set on a crisp autumn evening. Residents from all walks of life had gathered at the town hall, their hearts filled with warmth and determination for a cause close to their hearts—the annual charity event.

For weeks, volunteers had tirelessly worked to transform the town hall into a hub of activity and compassion. Tables adorned with colorful banners and bouquets of fresh flowers lined the spacious hall, setting the stage for an evening of generosity and goodwill.

Among the volunteers was Emma, a spirited young woman with a knack for organization and a heart as big as the event itself. She had rallied her friends and neighbors, inspiring them to donate their time and resources to make the charity event a resounding success.

As the doors swung open to welcome guests, the hall filled with laughter and chatter. Families mingled with local business owners, exchanging stories and admiring the array of items up for auction—a testament to the community's unwavering support for those in need.

Emma stood at the entrance, greeting guests with a warm smile and a welcoming embrace. She marveled at the sight of her town coming together, united in their commitment to make a difference. Each handshake and heartfelt conversation reinforced her belief in the power of collective action and kindness.

The evening kicked off with a heartfelt speech from Mayor Johnson, who praised the community's resilience and compassion. He spoke of the importance of standing together in times of hardship and extending a helping hand to those facing adversity—a sentiment that resonated deeply with everyone present.

As the auction began, excitement filled the air. Bids flew high as attendees vied for coveted items generously donated by local businesses—a weekend getaway at a rustic cabin, gourmet dinners at upscale restaurants, and handcrafted artworks that showcased the town's artistic talent.

In a corner of the hall, a children's play area buzzed with youthful energy. Volunteers had set up face-painting stations, storytelling corners, and a mini carnival with games and prizes. The sound of children's laughter echoed through the hall, a reminder of the joy that comes from giving back to the community.

Throughout the evening, guests enjoyed a delectable spread of hors d'oeuvres and beverages provided by the town's finest chefs and caterers. The aroma of freshly baked pastries and savory appetizers wafted through the air, tantalizing taste buds and fueling conversations about the event's impact on the community.

As the night progressed, Emma stole a moment to reflect on the journey that had brought them all together. She remembered the early mornings spent planning and organizing, the late nights coordinating with volunteers, and the moments of doubt overcome by the unwavering support of her neighbors.

The highlight of the evening came during the live appeal, where attendees were invited to pledge donations towards specific projects that would benefit local schools, healthcare facilities, and families in need. Emma watched with pride as pledges poured in, each one a testament to the generosity and compassion of Willowbrook's residents.

By the end of the night, the charity event had exceeded all expectations. The final tally revealed a staggering amount raised—an achievement that spoke volumes about the town's commitment to making a meaningful difference in the lives of others.

As guests bid farewell and dispersed into the night, Emma felt a profound sense of gratitude and fulfillment. The success of the charity event was not measured merely in dollars and cents, but in the bonds forged, the lives touched, and the spirit of community strengthened.

In the weeks that followed, Emma and her fellow volunteers continued to receive messages of thanks and appreciation from those who had benefited from their efforts. Stories emerged of scholarships awarded, medical treatments funded, and families supported during challenging times—a testament to the lasting impact of their collective generosity.

The charity event had not only brought financial relief to those in need but had also united the town of Willowbrook in a shared sense of purpose and compassion. It was a reminder that, when communities come together with kindness and determination, they can achieve extraordinary things.

As Emma looked forward to next year's event, she knew that the spirit of giving would continue to thrive in Willowbrook —a legacy of hope, compassion, and solidarity that would endure for years to come.

Anticipation - The feeling of excitement about something that is going to happen.

- The residents of Willowbrook were filled with anticipation as they prepared for the annual charity event, eager to make a difference in their community.

Resilience - The ability to recover quickly from difficulties; toughness.

- Mayor Johnson praised the community's resilience in his speech, highlighting how they had come together to support each other through challenging times.

Compassion - Sympathetic pity and concern for the sufferings or misfortunes of others.

- Emma's heart was filled with compassion as she greeted guests at the charity event, knowing their contributions would make a positive impact on people's lives.

Generosity - The quality of being kind, understanding, and not selfish; willingness to give money, help, or time freely.

- Local businesses showed their generosity by donating items for the auction, contributing to the success of the charity event.

Unwavering - Steady or resolute; not wavering.

- Emma's belief in the power of collective action and kindness was unwavering as she organized the charity event, despite the challenges they faced.

Tantalize - To tease or torment by presenting something desirable while keeping it out of reach.

- The aroma of freshly baked pastries tantalized the guests at the charity event, making their mouths water with anticipation.

Fulfillment - Satisfaction or happiness as a result of fully developing one's abilities or character.

- Emma felt a profound sense of fulfillment as she watched the community come together to support their neighbors in need.

Impact - The powerful effect that something, especially something new or different, has on a situation or person.

- The charity event had a significant impact on the lives of many in Willowbrook, providing essential resources and support where it was most needed.

Legacy - Something that is a part of your history or that remains from an earlier time.

- The spirit of giving and compassion created by the charity event would be a lasting legacy in Willowbrook, inspiring future generations to continue supporting their community.

Endure - To remain in existence; last.

- Emma knew that the legacy of hope and solidarity forged by the charity event would endure for years to come, benefiting the town of Willowbrook.

28.

THE MAGIC MIRROR

It was a lazy Sunday afternoon when Emily stumbled upon the dusty old mirror in the attic. The mirror, with its ornate frame and mysterious aura, had been hidden beneath layers of forgotten memories and childhood relics. As she wiped away the dust, a faint sparkle caught her eye, as if the mirror itself held a secret waiting to be revealed.

Curiosity piqued, Emily carried the mirror down to her bedroom and propped it up against the wall. She gazed into its reflective surface, half-expecting to see her own image staring back at her. Instead, she was met with a swirling mist that slowly coalesced into a vivid scene—a scene from the future.

In the mirror, Emily saw herself standing in a bustling city square, surrounded by towering skyscrapers and bustling crowds. She was dressed in a sleek business suit, clutching a leather-bound portfolio in one hand and confidently shaking hands with a group of executives. The scene filled her with a mixture of excitement and wonder—was this a glimpse of her future career success?

As quickly as it had appeared, the vision faded, leaving Emily staring at her own reflection once more. She blinked, unsure if what she had just witnessed was real or a figment of her imagination. But the tingling sensation in her fingertips and the lingering image in her mind told her otherwise.

Over the next few days, Emily found herself returning to the mirror, hoping to catch another glimpse of the future. Each time, the scenes were different yet equally captivating. In one vision, she saw herself standing on a sun-drenched beach, laughing with friends as they built sandcastles and splashed in the waves. In another, she witnessed herself receiving a prestigious award for her contributions to environmental conservation.

But not all the visions brought joy. In one unsettling glimpse, Emily saw herself sitting alone in a dimly lit room, tears streaming down her face as she clutched a crumpled letter in her hands. The scene filled her with an overwhelming sense of sadness and uncertainty—was this a warning of challenges yet to come?

As days turned into weeks, Emily's fascination with the magic mirror grew, but so did her apprehension. The visions, while mesmerizing, began to affect her daily life. She found herself preoccupied with thoughts of the future, wondering how much control she truly had over her destiny.

One evening, as Emily stood before the mirror once more, a new vision unfolded before her eyes. This time, she saw herself standing in a hospital room, holding a newborn baby in her arms. The room was filled with warmth and love, and Emily felt a surge of overwhelming joy and fulfillment. It was a moment of pure happiness, a glimpse of a future she had always dreamed of.

But just as quickly as the joy had come, it was overshadowed by a sense of doubt. What if the mirror was showing her only the good moments, hiding the challenges and hardships that lay ahead? Could she trust these visions to guide her decisions?

Lost in thought, Emily barely noticed her roommate, Sarah, entering the room. Sarah, always the practical one, had watched Emily's fascination with the mirror with a mixture of amusement and concern. She approached Emily with a gentle smile and sat down beside her.

"Emily, I've noticed you've been spending a lot of time with that mirror," Sarah said softly. "It's amazing what you're seeing, but remember, the future is uncertain. It's the present that matters most."

Emily sighed, torn between her fascination with the mirror and Sarah's wise words. "I know, but these visions feel so real, Sarah. They make me wonder if I'm on the right path, if I'm making the right choices."

Sarah nodded thoughtfully. "It's natural to seek guidance, especially when faced with uncertainty. But remember, the future is shaped by our actions in the present. The mirror might show possibilities, but it's up to us to create our own destiny."

Emily nodded, grateful for Sarah's perspective. She realized that while the mirror offered glimpses of what could be, it was ultimately her decisions and actions that would shape her future. With newfound resolve, she decided to focus on the present—to work hard, pursue her passions, and embrace the journey, wherever it might lead.

In the weeks that followed, Emily visited the mirror less frequently. She still cherished the glimpses it offered, but she no longer relied on them to define her path. Instead, she found joy in the everyday moments—studying for exams, spending time with friends, and pursuing her hobbies with passion and determination.

One evening, as Emily stood before the mirror, she saw a familiar scene—a reflection of herself, gazing into the mirror with a thoughtful expression. This time, there were no visions of the future, no swirling mists or vivid scenes. Just Emily, staring back at herself with a newfound sense of clarity and purpose.

As she turned away from the mirror, Emily knew that while the magic mirror had shown her glimpses of what could be, it was her own strength, resilience, and determination that would guide her journey. With a smile, she walked away, ready to embrace whatever the future held, one step at a time.

Anticipation - The feeling of excitement about something that is going to happen.

- Emily's anticipation grew as she approached the magic mirror, wondering what new vision she might see.

Fascination - The state of being extremely interested in something.

- Emily's fascination with the magic mirror intensified as she continued to see glimpses of her possible futures.

Uncertainty - The state of being unsure or not having confidence about the future.

- Emily felt a sense of uncertainty about the visions from the mirror, unsure if they were true glimpses of what lay ahead.

Resilience - The ability to recover quickly from difficulties; toughness.

- Emily's resilience was tested when she saw a troubling vision in the mirror, but she resolved to face whatever challenges came her way.

Overwhelming - Very intense or strong; overpowering.

- Emily felt an overwhelming sense of joy when she saw herself holding a newborn baby in one of the mirror's visions.

Apprehension - Anxiety or fear that something bad or unpleasant will happen.

- As the visions from the mirror became more frequent, Emily felt a growing sense of apprehension about their meaning.

Resolve - Firm determination to do something.

- With newfound resolve, Emily decided to focus on the present rather than becoming fixated on the mirror's visions.

Cherish - To value or care for something deeply.

- Emily learned to cherish the present moments in her life, rather than solely relying on visions of the future from the mirror.

Perspective - A particular attitude or way of regarding something; a point of view.

- Sarah offered Emily a new perspective on the visions from the mirror, encouraging her to focus on the present instead.

Clarity - The quality of being clear, coherent, or intelligible; clear understanding.

- After reflecting on Sarah's advice, Emily gained clarity about the role of the mirror in her life and how to approach its visions.

29.

A WINTER'S TALE

The snow fell softly outside, coating the world in a pristine blanket of white. Inside their cozy cottage nestled in the heart of the forest, the Johnson family gathered around the crackling fireplace, the warmth spreading comfort and cheer. It was Christmas Eve, and this year, they had decided to celebrate in a way that was both unique and meaningful.

"Mom, Dad, when can we start decorating the tree?" asked Emma, the youngest of the Johnson siblings, her eyes sparkling with excitement.

Mr. Johnson chuckled warmly. "Soon, sweetheart. Let's first enjoy a delicious breakfast together."

Mrs. Johnson, bustling about the kitchen, had prepared a feast fit for a holiday. The aroma of freshly baked cinnamon rolls filled the air, mingling with the scent of pine from the Christmas tree waiting to be adorned with ornaments and lights.

As they sat down to eat, Mr. Johnson began the tradition of sharing stories from past winters. "Do you remember the year we had that big snowstorm, and we built an igloo in the backyard?" he reminisced, a twinkle in his eye.

"Yeah! And we all slept in it overnight!" exclaimed Ben, the eldest, his voice filled with nostalgia.

The family laughed and exchanged fond memories, savoring each moment of togetherness. After breakfast, they gathered around the tree, a majestic fir adorned with twinkling lights and colorful baubles. Christmas carols played softly in the background, filling the room with joyous melodies.

"Now, who's ready to open presents?" Mrs. Johnson announced with a smile, handing out carefully wrapped gifts to each family member.

Emma eagerly tore into her presents, squealing with delight as she uncovered a new set of art supplies and a book she had been longing to read. Ben unwrapped a sleek new camera, a thoughtful gift to support his passion for photography. Mr. and Mrs. Johnson exchanged gifts—a cozy sweater for her and a set of gourmet coffee blends for him, perfect for their quiet mornings together.

Once the presents were opened and the excitement subsided, Mr. Johnson suggested they take a walk in the snowy woods. "It's a tradition in some cultures to connect with nature on Christmas Day," he explained.

The family bundled up in scarves and mittens, their boots crunching through the freshly fallen snow as they wandered deeper into the forest. The sun peeked through the clouds, casting a golden glow over the winter landscape. They stumbled upon a frozen pond, its surface shimmering like a mirror under the pale winter sun.

As they walked, Emma noticed a small, abandoned bird's nest nestled in the branches of a tree. "Look, Dad! Do you think the birds will come back in the spring?" she asked, her breath forming wispy clouds in the chilly air.

Mr. Johnson knelt beside her, brushing the snow off the nest gently. "I think so, sweetheart. Nature has a way of coming back to life, even after the coldest winters."

They continued their stroll, marveling at the beauty of the winter wonderland around them. The forest seemed to hold its breath, as if waiting in anticipation for the magic that the season brought.

Back at the cottage, Mrs. Johnson prepared a hearty lunch of warm soup and crusty bread. They gathered around the table once more, sharing stories of their adventure in the woods and planning the rest of their day.

"Let's make hot cocoa and watch a holiday movie later," suggested Ben, a contented smile on his face.

"That sounds perfect," agreed Mrs. Johnson, pouring steaming mugs of cocoa for everyone.

As the afternoon sun dipped below the horizon, casting long shadows across the snow-covered landscape, the Johnson family settled in front of the fireplace once more. The crackling fire danced and flickered, casting a warm glow over their faces as they watched a classic holiday film together.

In the quiet moments between scenes, Emma leaned against her mother, feeling a deep sense of gratitude and love for her family. They had created their own unique winter celebration, filled with warmth, laughter, and cherished traditions.

As the credits rolled and the fire burned low, Mr. Johnson spoke softly, breaking the peaceful silence. "This has been a special Christmas, hasn't it? Different from our usual celebrations, but just as memorable."

"Absolutely," agreed Mrs. Johnson, her voice filled with warmth. "It's shown us that the spirit of the holidays isn't just about the traditions we follow—it's about the love we share and the moments we create together."

Emma nodded sleepily, her eyelids growing heavy with the warmth of the fire and the comfort of her family's presence. As she drifted off to sleep, nestled in the embrace of her loved ones, she knew that this winter's tale would be one she would cherish for years to come.

Cozy - Giving a feeling of comfort, warmth, and relaxation.

- The Johnson family gathered around the cozy fireplace, enjoying the crackling fire and each other's company.

Majestic - Having impressive beauty or scale.

- The Christmas tree stood tall and majestic in the corner of the room, adorned with twinkling lights and colorful ornaments.

Adorn - To decorate or add beauty to something.

- The Johnsons adorned the Christmas tree with handmade ornaments and strings of sparkling lights.

Nostalgia - A sentimental longing or affection for the past.

- Ben's voice was filled with nostalgia as he reminisced about building an igloo during a past winter.

Hearty - Satisfying and substantial, especially regarding food.

- Mrs. Johnson prepared a hearty lunch of soup and crusty bread for the family after their walk in the snowy woods.

Bundle up - To dress warmly, especially in layers, to protect against cold weather.

- The Johnsons bundled up in scarves and mittens before venturing out into the snowy forest for their Christmas walk.

Glimmer - A faint or unsteady light; to shine faintly.

- The frozen pond's surface glimmered like a mirror under the winter sun, reflecting the golden light.

Anticipation - The feeling of excitement about something that is going to happen.

- Emma's anticipation grew as she waited to open her

Christmas presents with her family by the cozy fireplace.

Crust - The crisp and firm outer layer of bread or baked goods.

- Mrs. Johnson served crusty bread alongside the warm soup for lunch, which was perfect on a cold winter day.

Embrace - To accept or support something willingly and enthusiastically.

- The Johnson family embraced their unique Christmas celebration, filled with warmth, laughter, and cherished traditions.

30.

THE HIDDEN TREASURE

On a warm summer afternoon, Tim and his younger sister, Sarah, stumbled upon an old, dusty box in the attic of their grandparents' house. It was a Saturday, and they had been exploring every nook and cranny of the ancient house, trying to uncover its secrets.

"Look, Sarah! I found something!" Tim exclaimed, his eyes wide with excitement as he lifted the lid of the box. Inside, nestled among yellowed newspapers and faded photographs, was an intricately drawn map.

"What is it, Tim?" Sarah asked, peering over his shoulder with curiosity.

"It looks like a treasure map!" Tim replied, his voice filled with awe. "See these markings? They seem to point to a spot in the woods behind the old mill."

Sarah's eyes widened in wonder. "Do you think there's really treasure buried there?"

Tim shrugged, a grin spreading across his face. "There's only one way to find out. Let's go on an adventure!"

With that, they carefully folded the map and tucked it into Tim's backpack. They raced downstairs, eager to share their discovery with Grandma and Grandpa.

"Look what we found!" Sarah exclaimed, waving the map in

front of their grandparents.

Grandma peered at the map through her spectacles, her eyes twinkling with amusement. "Ah, the old treasure map! Your grandfather and I used to pretend to search for treasure when we were your age."

"Is it real, Grandma? Can we really find treasure?" Tim asked eagerly, his excitement palpable.

Grandpa chuckled warmly, ruffling Tim's hair affectionately. "Well, you never know. Sometimes, the greatest treasures are the memories you make along the way."

Undeterred by their grandparents' playful skepticism, Tim and Sarah spent the rest of the afternoon planning their expedition. They packed sandwiches, water bottles, and a flashlight—just in case they needed to explore dark caves or hidden tunnels.

As the sun began to set, casting a golden hue over the horizon, Tim and Sarah set off into the woods behind the old mill. The air was filled with the chirping of crickets and the rustling of leaves as they followed the map's instructions, crossing babbling brooks and climbing over fallen logs.

"According to the map, the treasure should be buried near that big oak tree," Tim whispered excitedly, pointing ahead.

They approached the towering oak tree, its gnarled branches reaching towards the sky like ancient fingers. Tim knelt down and began to dig in the soft earth, his heart racing with anticipation. Sarah watched eagerly, holding her breath in anticipation.

After what felt like hours of digging, Tim's shovel hit something hard. With a triumphant shout, he unearthed a rusty metal box buried just beneath the surface.

"We found it, Sarah! We found the treasure!" Tim exclaimed,

his eyes wide with disbelief and joy.

Together, they carefully lifted the lid of the box. Inside, nestled among worn coins and glittering jewels, was a collection of old photographs and handwritten letters tied with a faded ribbon.

Sarah picked up one of the letters, her hands trembling slightly. "What do they say, Tim?"

Tim unfolded the letter and read aloud, his voice filled with wonder. "To whomever finds this treasure: These are the memories of a lifetime—a love story that spans generations. May you cherish them as much as we have."

Tears welled up in Sarah's eyes as she looked at the photographs—faded images of a couple dancing under the stars, children playing in a sunlit garden, and a family gathered around a roaring fireplace.

"They're beautiful," Sarah whispered, her voice filled with emotion.

Tim nodded solemnly, his heart touched by the stories captured in those old photographs. "This is the real treasure, Sarah. These memories—they're priceless."

As the sun dipped below the horizon, casting a warm glow over the clearing, Tim and Sarah carefully reburied the box, leaving the treasure undisturbed for future explorers to discover. Hand in hand, they walked back through the woods, their hearts full of wonder and gratitude for the adventure they had shared.

Back at their grandparents' house, they shared their story over a hearty dinner with Grandma and Grandpa. The evening passed in a blur of laughter and storytelling, each of them savoring the magic of that unforgettable day.

As they climbed into bed that night, Tim and Sarah knew that they had experienced something truly special. The hidden treasure they had uncovered wasn't just gold and jewels—it was a journey of discovery, love, and the enduring bond between siblings.

And as they drifted off to sleep, their dreams were filled with visions of future adventures, waiting to be explored.

Intricately - In a detailed and complex manner.

- Inside the old box, they found an intricately drawn map that seemed to lead to a hidden treasure.

Palpable - Easily perceived; noticeable.

- Tim's excitement was palpable as they followed the treasure map into the woods behind the old mill.

Skepticism - Doubt about the truth or validity of something.

- Despite their grandparents' skepticism about finding real treasure, Tim and Sarah were determined to follow the map.

Triumphant - Feeling or showing great happiness or victory.

- With a triumphant shout, Tim unearthed the rusty metal box buried near the oak tree.

Unearth - To dig up something that has been buried.

- After hours of digging, they unearthed a treasure chest filled with old photographs and letters.

Tremble - To shake involuntarily, typically as a result of excitement or fear.

- Sarah's hands trembled slightly as she picked up one of the old letters from the treasure chest.

Solemnly - In a serious and thoughtful manner.

- Tim nodded solemnly as they read aloud the heartfelt

messages written in the old letters they found.

Enduring - Lasting over a long period of time; continuing.

- The hidden treasure represented the enduring love and memories of a family through generations.

Undisturbed - Not interrupted or interfered with; left in peace.

- Tim and Sarah carefully reburied the treasure box, leaving it undisturbed for future explorers to discover.

Unforgettable - Impossible to forget; very memorable.

- The day they found the hidden treasure in the woods became an unforgettable experience for Tim and Sarah.

31.

THE NEW NEIGHBOR

It was a sunny Saturday morning when the Johnson family noticed the moving truck pulling up next door. Excitement buzzed through their quiet suburban street as neighbors peeked out from behind curtains and gathered on front porches to catch a glimpse of the newcomers.

"I wonder who's moving in," Mrs. Johnson mused, sipping her morning coffee from the kitchen window.

"I hope they have kids around our age," Tommy, the Johnsons' ten-year-old son, chimed in eagerly. "It'd be cool to have someone to play basketball with."

Mr. Johnson nodded thoughtfully, setting down his newspaper. "New neighbors can bring a lot of changes, Tommy. Let's give them a warm welcome."

As if on cue, a car pulled into the driveway next door, and a family of four emerged—a mom, dad, and two children around Tommy's age. They began unloading boxes and furniture while Tommy watched from his bedroom window with growing anticipation.

Later that afternoon, Mrs. Johnson knocked on the new neighbors' door with a plate of freshly baked cookies in hand. She was greeted by Mrs. Patel, the mother of the family, who welcomed her with a warm smile.

"Hello, I'm Lisa Johnson from next door," Mrs. Johnson introduced herself cheerfully, holding out the plate of cookies. "We wanted to welcome you to the neighborhood!"

Mrs. Patel's face lit up with gratitude as she accepted the cookies. "Thank you so much, Lisa! I'm Pooja Patel, and this is my husband, Sanjay." She gestured towards her husband, who was busy carrying in a large box.

"We're so glad to meet you," Mrs. Patel continued, her accent adding a touch of charm to her words. "And these are our children, Maya and Rohan."

Tommy shyly waved from behind his mother, earning a friendly smile from Maya and Rohan.

"Would you like to come in for some tea?" Mrs. Patel offered warmly. "We haven't finished unpacking yet, but we'd love to chat."

Mrs. Johnson nodded eagerly, stepping into the Patel's cozy living room. The air was filled with the scent of fresh paint and moving boxes, but Mrs. Johnson could already sense a feeling of warmth and hospitality in the air.

Over tea and cookies, the two families exchanged stories and got to know each other better. The Patels had recently moved from a big city to pursue new job opportunities and to give their children a quieter, more family-oriented lifestyle.

"We were a bit nervous about moving to a new place," Mr. Patel admitted with a chuckle, "but everyone here has been so welcoming. It already feels like home."

As the afternoon turned into evening, Tommy and Rohan disappeared into the backyard, bonding over their shared love for video games and superheroes. Maya and Mrs. Johnson chatted about their favorite books and movies, discovering common interests that made them fast friends.

In the weeks that followed, the Johnsons and the Patels became inseparable. They attended neighborhood barbecues together, organized playdates for the children, and even started a community garden project.

With Mrs. Patel's background in urban planning, she proposed turning a vacant lot at the end of the street into a vibrant community garden. Everyone loved the idea, and soon, weekends were filled with digging, planting, and laughter as neighbors of all ages came together to create something beautiful.

The garden became a symbol of unity and friendship in the neighborhood, attracting attention from local media and inspiring other communities to start similar projects.

"It's amazing how one family can make such a big difference," Mrs. Johnson remarked one evening, admiring the blooming flowers and bustling activity in the garden.

Mr. Patel nodded proudly, wiping his brow after a long day of gardening. "We feel so lucky to have found such wonderful neighbors. This community has welcomed us with open arms."

As the seasons changed, so did the neighborhood. Children's laughter echoed through the streets, and friendships blossomed like the flowers in the garden. The Patels had indeed brought exciting changes to the community—not just with their ideas and enthusiasm, but with their kindness and willingness to connect.

And as Tommy and Rohan raced down the street on their bikes, their laughter echoing into the sunset, the Johnsons knew that their new neighbors had become cherished friends—a testament to the power of welcoming hearts and open minds in creating a vibrant, close-knit community.

Anticipation - A feeling of excitement about something that is going to happen.

- Tommy watched from his bedroom window with growing anticipation as the new neighbors unloaded their belongings.

Hospitality - Friendly and generous reception and entertainment of guests, visitors, or strangers.

- Mrs. Patel welcomed Mrs. Johnson into their home with warmth and hospitality, offering tea and cookies.

Chuckled - Laughed quietly or to oneself.

- Mr. Patel chuckled when he recalled their initial nervousness about moving to the neighborhood.

Unity - The state of being united or joined as a whole.

- The community garden project became a symbol of unity as neighbors worked together to create something beautiful.

Enthusiasm - Intense and eager enjoyment, interest, or approval.

- The Patels brought enthusiasm to the neighborhood, sparking excitement with their ideas for community projects.

Vibrant - Full of energy and life; bright and striking.

- The neighborhood became more vibrant with the laughter of children and the blossoming of friendships.

Symbol - A thing that represents or stands for something else, especially a material object representing something abstract.

- The garden became a symbol of friendship and community spirit in the neighborhood.

Cherished - To value or care for something deeply.

- The Johnsons cherished their newfound friendship with the Patels, grateful for their warmth and kindness.

Open-minded - Willing to consider new ideas; unprejudiced.

- The community embraced the Patels' ideas for the garden project, showing that they were open-minded and eager for positive change.

Blossomed - Developed or grew in a healthy or vigorous way.

- Friendships blossomed among the neighbors as they worked together on various community initiatives.

32.

THE PERFECT GARDEN

In the quiet suburb of Willow Grove, nestled between tall oaks and blooming azaleas, lived a woman named Emily who had a passion for gardening. Her backyard was a colorful tapestry of roses, lilies, and sunflowers, each petal meticulously cared for and nurtured. Emily's love for gardening began when she was just a child, helping her grandmother tend to the flowers in their small, sunny garden.

One crisp spring morning, Emily received a letter that would change her gardening journey forever. It was an invitation to participate in the annual Green Thumb Gardening Competition, a prestigious event known for showcasing the most exquisite gardens in the region. Excitement bubbled inside her as she read the details—the categories, the judges, and the coveted prize: a rare collection of heirloom seeds.

"I can't believe it!" Emily exclaimed, waving the letter in the air. "I've always dreamed of entering this competition."

Her husband, Mark, grinned from the kitchen table where he was enjoying his morning coffee. "You've worked so hard on our garden, Emily. It's about time you got recognized for it."

With newfound determination, Emily spent every spare moment preparing her garden for the competition. She weeded, pruned, and fertilized, ensuring that each flower and shrub was at its peak of perfection. She researched gardening techniques, consulted with local experts, and even experimented with new plant varieties to add a touch of uniqueness to her garden.

As the competition day drew near, Emily's excitement grew palpable. The morning of the event dawned bright and clear, with a gentle breeze carrying the scent of freshly cut grass and blooming flowers. Emily carefully loaded her prized plants into the car, along with a notebook detailing each plant's care and history.

Arriving at the competition venue—a sprawling botanical garden with manicured lawns and towering topiaries—Emily was greeted by a buzz of activity. Gardeners of all ages and backgrounds bustled about, arranging their displays and nervously adjusting flower pots.

"I can't believe how beautiful everything looks," Emily whispered to herself, awestruck by the array of colors and scents that surrounded her.

She set up her garden display in a quiet corner under the shade of an old oak tree. Her roses stood tall and vibrant, their petals a rich shade of crimson. Beside them, delicate lavender danced in the breeze, its soothing aroma filling the air. Emily arranged her plants with care, ensuring that each one complemented the others in a harmonious symphony of colors and textures.

As the judging began, Emily's nerves fluttered like butterflies in her stomach. She watched anxiously as the judges, a panel of seasoned gardeners and horticulturists, examined each garden with keen eyes and thoughtful expressions. They measured plant heights, evaluated flower health, and even took note of the symmetry and layout of each display.

Hours passed in a blur of anticipation and excitement. Emily mingled with other participants, exchanging gardening tips and stories of their favorite blooms. She marveled at the passion and dedication that each gardener poured into their creations, realizing that she was among kindred spirits who shared her love for gardening.

Finally, the moment of truth arrived. The judges gathered around a wooden table, their faces serious yet thoughtful. Emily held her breath as they deliberated, their voices hushed and muffled by the rustling leaves overhead.

"And the winner of this year's Green Thumb Gardening Competition is..." announced Mr. Thompson, the head judge, his voice echoing across the garden.

Emily's heart skipped a beat as she listened with bated breath. She glanced nervously at her garden, hoping against hope that her hard work and dedication had paid off.

"Emily Johnson, for her outstanding display of creativity, passion, and horticultural skill!" Mr. Thompson declared, his voice filled with admiration.

Cheers erupted from the crowd as Emily stood frozen in disbelief. She had won! Tears welled up in her eyes as she stepped forward to receive her prize—a beautiful bouquet of flowers and the coveted collection of heirloom seeds.

"I can't believe it," Emily murmured, her voice trembling with emotion. "Thank you so much."

Mark rushed forward to envelope her in a tight hug, his pride shining in his eyes. "You did it, Emily! You created the perfect garden."

But as Emily looked around at the gardens of her fellow competitors, she realized something important. Each garden, whether wild and whimsical or meticulously manicured, reflected its creator's unique vision and passion for plants. The true beauty of the competition lay not in winning, but in celebrating the diversity and creativity of gardening.

With a heart full of gratitude and a newfound sense of fulfillment, Emily knew that her journey as a gardener was far from over. The Green Thumb Gardening Competition had taught her that true beauty lies not in perfection, but in the love and dedication poured into every leaf, petal, and stem.

And as she drove home with her prize and a heart full of joy, Emily couldn't wait to continue nurturing her garden, knowing that each bloom was a testament to her passion for plants and the beauty they brought into her life.

Exquisite - Extremely beautiful and, typically, delicate.

o   The Green Thumb Gardening Competition showcased the most exquisite gardens in the region, each one a masterpiece of floral artistry.

Palpable - Able to be touched or felt; easily perceptible.

o   Emily's excitement before the competition was palpable as she carefully prepared her garden for display.

Manicured - (of a garden or lawn) trimmed and maintained to a tidy and neat appearance.

o   The botanical garden where the competition took place was filled with manicured lawns and meticulously pruned topiaries.

Symphony - A complex musical composition, typically with orchestral instruments, expressing deep feelings or emotions.

o   Emily arranged her plants in her garden display like a symphony, ensuring that each one contributed harmoniously to the overall composition.

Deliberated - Engaged in long and careful consideration.

o   The judges deliberated over each garden display,

evaluating every detail from plant health to layout and design.

Coveted - Eagerly desired or wished for.

o   Emily's prize for winning the competition included a coveted collection of heirloom seeds, which she had dreamed of planting in her garden.

Enveloped - Completely surrounded or covered.

o   Mark rushed forward and enveloped Emily in a tight hug after she was announced as the winner of the competition.

Whimsical - Playfully quaint or fanciful, especially in an appealing and amusing way.

o   Emily noticed that some of the gardens in the competition were whimsical, featuring unconventional plant arrangements and decorations.

Fulfilled - Satisfied or happy because of fully developing one's abilities or character.

o   Winning the competition left Emily with a sense of fulfillment, knowing that her hard work and dedication had paid off.

Nurturing - Caring for and encouraging the growth or development of someone or something.

o   Emily couldn't wait to continue nurturing her garden after the competition, knowing that each bloom was a testament to her love for gardening.

33.

THE MYSTERY OF
THE BROKEN VASE

Detective Sarah Holmes strode through the grand entrance of Winston Manor, her eyes scanning the opulent surroundings. Crystal chandeliers hung from the ceiling, casting shimmering reflections on the marble floor below. Portraits of stern-faced ancestors lined the walls, their eyes seemingly following her every move.

Sarah had been called to Winston Manor to investigate a peculiar incident—the mysterious shattering of a priceless Ming Dynasty vase that had adorned the foyer for generations. The owners, Mr. and Mrs. Winston, stood anxiously by the broken pieces, their faces etched with concern.

"Thank you for coming, Detective Holmes," Mr. Winston said, his voice trembling slightly. "We're at a loss as to how this could have happened."

Sarah nodded reassuringly. "I'll do my best to get to the bottom of this mystery."

She crouched down beside the shattered vase, examining the pieces with a keen eye. The vase, adorned with delicate blue and white patterns, lay in fragments on the floor. Sarah noted the absence of any obvious signs of forced entry or struggle nearby.

"Can you tell me what happened?" Sarah asked, looking up at the Winstons.

Mrs. Winston wrung her hands nervously. "We were hosting a small dinner party last night," she explained. "Everything was going smoothly until we heard a loud crash from the foyer. When we rushed in, we found the vase like this."

Mr. Winston nodded in agreement. "None of our guests were near the vase when it broke. It's as if it shattered on its own."

Sarah stood up and surveyed the room thoughtfully. "Do you mind if I speak with your guests? Sometimes, even the smallest detail can be crucial in solving a case."

The Winstons exchanged a hesitant glance before nodding. Sarah spent the next hour interviewing the dinner guests—a mix of friends, business associates, and distant relatives. Each person recounted their movements and activities leading up to the moment the vase broke.

As Sarah listened attentively, she pieced together a timeline of events. Mrs. Winston had been in the dining room, overseeing the serving of dessert. Mr. Winston had excused himself to take an important phone call in his study. The guests, meanwhile, had engaged in lively conversation in the drawing-room adjacent to the foyer.

One guest, in particular, caught Sarah's attention—Dr. Samantha Hayes, a renowned archaeologist and a longtime friend of the Winstons. Dr. Hayes had been examining a nearby painting when the vase shattered, and her alibi seemed solid. Yet, Sarah couldn't shake the feeling that there was more to the story.

Returning to the foyer, Sarah knelt down once more beside the broken vase. She inspected the pieces meticulously, noting the angle at which they had fallen and the pattern of cracks on the floor. Then, something caught her eye—a faint smudge of dirt on one of the broken shards.

"Interesting," Sarah muttered to herself, pulling a small

evidence bag from her pocket to collect the shard.

Just then, a soft cough interrupted her concentration. It was Dr. Hayes, standing at the entrance to the foyer with a curious expression on her face.

"Detective Holmes, may I speak with you for a moment?" Dr. Hayes asked, her voice tinged with concern.

Sarah straightened up, holding the evidence bag behind her back. "Of course, Dr. Hayes. What can I help you with?"

Dr. Hayes hesitated for a moment before speaking. "I couldn't help but notice your interest in that shard of the vase. Is there something you've discovered?"

Sarah regarded Dr. Hayes carefully. "It's possible," she replied cryptically. "I'm still piecing together the evidence."

Dr. Hayes nodded thoughtfully. "Well, if there's anything I can do to assist your investigation, please don't hesitate to ask. I'm here to help in any way I can."

With that, Dr. Hayes turned and walked back toward the drawing-room, leaving Sarah to ponder her words. Could Dr. Hayes be hiding something? Sarah wondered. Or was she genuinely concerned about the investigation?

Determined to uncover the truth, Sarah continued her examination of the scene. She analyzed the dirt sample from the vase shard under a microscope in her makeshift mobile lab. The dirt turned out to be a rare blend found only in one specific region—near the Winston Manor.

The pieces of the puzzle were slowly coming together in Sarah's mind. She retraced Dr. Hayes's movements during the dinner party and realized that she had been near the vase just moments before it broke. Could Dr. Hayes have accidentally knocked over the vase, then cleverly concealed her involvement?

Sarah confronted Dr. Hayes in the drawing-room, presenting her with the evidence—the shard with the dirt sample.

"Dr. Hayes, I believe you were near the vase when it broke," Sarah stated firmly.

Dr. Hayes's eyes widened in surprise, but then she sighed deeply, her shoulders slumping in defeat. "You're right, Detective Holmes. I was examining the vase when I accidentally knocked it over. I panicked and left the scene before anyone noticed."

Sarah nodded, her expression sympathetic. "Thank you for being honest, Dr. Hayes. Accidents happen, but it's important to take responsibility for our actions."

Dr. Hayes apologized profusely to the Winstons, who accepted her apology with grace and understanding. They were relieved that the mystery of the broken vase had been solved, even if it meant their valuable Ming Dynasty artifact was irreparably damaged.

As Sarah prepared to leave Winston Manor, Mr. Winston approached her with a small token of appreciation—a delicate porcelain figurine of a detective solving a mystery.

"Thank you, Detective Holmes," Mr. Winston said warmly. "You've restored peace of mind to our home."

Sarah accepted the figurine with a smile. "It was my pleasure, Mr. Winston. Just another day in the life of a detective."

And with that, Sarah Holmes bid farewell to Winston Manor, her mind already racing with thoughts of her next case and the mysteries yet to be solved.

Opulent - Luxurious and costly, characterized by grandeur.

- Sarah Holmes entered Winston Manor, taking in the opulent surroundings of crystal chandeliers and marble floors.

Anxiously - In a nervous or worried manner.

- Mr. and Mrs. Winston stood anxiously by the broken vase, concerned about its mysterious shattering.

Peculiar - Strange or unusual, especially in a way that is unsettling.

- Detective Holmes was called to investigate the peculiar incident of the broken Ming Dynasty vase at Winston Manor.

Reassuringly - In a way that alleviates someone's fears or concerns.

- Sarah nodded reassuringly to Mr. Winston, promising to solve the mystery of the broken vase.

Meticulously - In a way that shows great attention to detail; very thoroughly.

- Sarah examined the shattered vase meticulously, searching for clues that could explain its sudden breakage.

Hesitant - Unsure or slow to act or speak.

- The Winstons exchanged a hesitant glance before agreeing to let Sarah interview their dinner guests.

Cryptically - In a mysterious or obscure way, often intentionally.

- Sarah replied cryptically to Dr. Hayes, keeping her suspicions about the broken vase shard to herself.

Sympathetic - Showing empathy or understanding towards someone's feelings or situation.

- Sarah's expression was sympathetic when Dr. Hayes confessed to accidentally breaking the vase.

Profusely - To a great degree; in large amounts.

- Dr. Hayes apologized profusely to the Winstons for her role in breaking the Ming Dynasty vase.

Grace - Elegance or beauty of movement, form, or manner.

- The Winstons accepted Dr. Hayes's apology with grace and understanding, despite the irreparable damage to their prized vase.

34.

THE LITTLE BAKERY

Nestled between two bustling streets in the heart of Brookside Avenue, the aroma of freshly baked bread and sweet pastries wafted through the air from a small, unassuming bakery. The Little Bakery, as it was affectionately called by locals, had become much more than just a place to pick up morning croissants or afternoon treats. It had woven itself into the very fabric of the neighborhood, becoming a beloved gathering spot where stories were shared, friendships were forged, and memories were made.

The bakery was run by Mr. and Mrs. Thompson, a couple who had always dreamed of owning their own business. With their passion for baking and unwavering determination, they had transformed a quaint little shop into a bustling hub of activity. From the moment they opened their doors each morning, customers streamed in, drawn not only by the tantalizing smells but also by the warm welcome and friendly chatter that filled the air.

One brisk autumn morning, as the sun painted the sky with hues of gold and crimson, a new customer walked through the bakery's door. Her name was Emily, a recent transplant to the neighborhood, who had heard whispers of the bakery's delectable delights from her neighbors. As she stepped inside, she was greeted by the sight of shelves brimming with crusty loaves of bread, rows of colorful cupcakes adorned with swirls of frosting, and trays of buttery croissants that seemed to melt in the mouth.

"Welcome to The Little Bakery," Mrs. Thompson said with a

bright smile, wiping her flour-dusted hands on her apron. "What can I get for you today?"

Emily glanced at the array of treats, her mouth watering at the sight. "Everything looks so delicious," she replied, her eyes lighting up. "I think I'll start with a cinnamon roll and a cup of coffee, please."

Mrs. Thompson nodded warmly and set about preparing Emily's order. As Emily waited, she couldn't help but notice the sense of community that permeated the bakery. Regular customers greeted each other with familiar nods and exchanged pleasantries about the weather or the latest neighborhood news. Children darted around, their faces sticky with frosting as they savored their favorite treats.

Once her order was ready, Emily took a seat by the window, savoring the warmth of her coffee and the indulgent sweetness of the cinnamon roll. She watched as a group of elderly friends gathered at a nearby table, their laughter echoing off the bakery's cozy walls. They shared stories of days gone by, reminiscing about their own childhoods and the joys of growing up in the neighborhood.

As weeks turned into months, Emily found herself becoming a regular at The Little Bakery. It wasn't just the delicious pastries that kept drawing her back—it was the sense of belonging that she felt every time she stepped through the door. She struck up conversations with other customers, learning about their lives and forging new friendships along the way.

One rainy afternoon, Emily found herself in need of a pick-me-up after a particularly long day at work. She ducked into The Little Bakery, the familiar scent of freshly baked bread wrapping around her like a comforting hug. Mrs. Thompson greeted her with a sympathetic smile and handed her a steaming mug of hot chocolate and a slice of homemade apple pie.

"Rough day?" Mrs. Thompson asked gently, her eyes full of understanding.

Emily nodded gratefully, taking a sip of the rich hot chocolate. "It feels like everything's going wrong," she admitted. "But being here, surrounded by warmth and kindness—it makes everything a little bit better."

Mrs. Thompson patted Emily's hand reassuringly. "You're always welcome here, Emily," she said sincerely. "The bakery isn't just about serving food—it's about nourishing the soul and creating connections."

Those words stayed with Emily as she sat in the cozy warmth of The Little Bakery, watching the rain patter against the window. She realized that the bakery wasn't just a place to satisfy her sweet tooth—it was a sanctuary, a place where she could find solace and support during life's ups and downs.

Months turned into years, and The Little Bakery continued to thrive, its reputation spreading far and wide. It became a gathering place for celebrations—birthdays, anniversaries, and even impromptu parties. Mr. and Mrs. Thompson expanded their menu to include new creations inspired by customer suggestions, ensuring that there was always something new and exciting to try.

One sunny spring morning, as Emily sipped her coffee outside The Little Bakery, she marveled at how much the small shop had come to mean to her and the entire neighborhood. It wasn't just a bakery anymore—it was a cornerstone of community life, a place where people of all ages and backgrounds came together to share moments of joy, comfort, and connection.

As she took another bite of her favorite almond croissant, Emily couldn't help but smile. The Little Bakery had indeed become the heart of the neighborhood—a testament to the power of good food, warm hospitality, and the simple joy of coming together.

And in that moment, Emily knew that no matter where life took her, The Little Bakery would always hold a special place in her heart.

Bustling - Full of energetic and noisy activity.

- The Little Bakery was a bustling hub of activity every morning, with customers streaming in for freshly baked pastries.

Indulgent - Allowing oneself to enjoy the pleasure of something, especially food or drink, in large quantities.

- Emily savored the indulgent sweetness of the cinnamon roll she ordered at The Little Bakery.

Cozy - Giving a feeling of comfort, warmth, and relaxation.

- The elderly friends enjoyed their afternoon at The Little Bakery, sitting at a cozy table by the window.

Solace - Comfort or consolation in a time of distress or sadness.

- Emily found solace in the warm atmosphere and kindness of The Little Bakery after a rough day at work.

Sanctuary - A place of refuge or safety; a peaceful and safe haven.

- The Little Bakery had become a sanctuary for Emily, where she could relax and unwind after a stressful day.

Impromptu - Done without being planned or rehearsed; spontaneous.

- The Little Bakery often hosted impromptu parties for customers celebrating special occasions.

Cornerstone - An essential or fundamental part of something.

- The Little Bakery had become a cornerstone of community life, bringing people together from all walks of life.

Marveled - To be filled with wonder or astonishment.

- Emily marveled at how The Little Bakery had grown to mean so much to her and the entire neighborhood.

Testament - Something that serves as a sign or evidence of a specified fact, event, or quality.

- The success of The Little Bakery was a testament to the dedication and hard work of Mr. and Mrs. Thompson.

Hospitality - The friendly and generous reception and entertainment of guests, visitors, or strangers.

- Mrs. Thompson's warm hospitality made The Little Bakery not just a place to eat, but a place to feel welcomed and cared for.

35.

THE UNEXPECTED PROPOSAL

Emma sat in her favorite coffee shop, watching the rain fall outside. It had been a long week at work, and she was grateful for this moment of peace. She took a sip of her latte and looked around the cozy cafe. The familiar faces of the baristas and the regular customers brought a sense of comfort. Little did she know, today would be a day she would never forget.

As she glanced at the door, she saw Liam, her boyfriend of three years, walk in. He was soaked from the rain, but he had a big smile on his face. Emma waved at him, and he made his way over to her table.

"Hey, you," Liam said, leaning down to give her a quick kiss. "Mind if I join you?"

"Of course not," Emma replied, moving her bag to make room for him. "How was your day?"

"It was busy, but I have some exciting news," Liam said, sitting down across from her. He reached into his bag and pulled out a small, gift-wrapped box.

Emma's eyes widened. "What's this for? It's not my birthday, and Christmas is months away."

Liam chuckled. "I know, but I couldn't wait. Open it."

With curiosity, Emma untied the ribbon and carefully unwrapped the box. Inside was a delicate silver necklace with a heart-shaped pendant. She looked up at Liam, her eyes shining.

"It's beautiful, Liam. Thank you so much," she said, touched by the thoughtful gift.

"There's more," Liam said, his voice suddenly serious. He reached across the table and took her hand. "Emma, you are the most amazing person I know. These past three years with you have been the best of my life. I want to spend the rest of my life with you."

Emma's heart started to race. She had dreamed about this moment but never expected it to happen here, in their favorite coffee shop, on a rainy afternoon.

Liam got down on one knee and pulled out a small velvet box. He opened it to reveal a beautiful diamond ring. "Emma, will you marry me?"

Tears filled Emma's eyes as she nodded. "Yes, Liam, I will!" she said, her voice trembling with emotion.

The coffee shop erupted in applause. The baristas cheered, and the customers clapped, some wiping away their own tears. Liam slipped the ring onto Emma's finger and stood up, pulling her into a tight embrace.

They sat back down, their hands still intertwined. "I can't believe this is happening," Emma said, looking at the ring sparkling on her finger.

"Believe it, because it's real," Liam said with a grin. "I love you, Emma."

"I love you too, Liam," she replied, her heart full of joy.

They spent the rest of the afternoon talking about their future, making plans for the wedding, and imagining their life together. Emma felt a sense of happiness and excitement she had never felt before. She knew that no matter what challenges they might face, they would face them together.

Later that evening, they walked home in the rain, not caring that they were getting soaked. They were too busy dreaming about the life they were going to build together.

As they reached Emma's apartment, Liam stopped and looked at her. "You know, I wanted to propose to you in a fancy restaurant, but I realized that our love is not about fancy things. It's about the simple, everyday moments we share. Like this one, walking home in the rain."

Emma smiled. "I wouldn't have it any other way," she said. "This is perfect."

They went inside, and Emma made hot chocolate while Liam lit some candles. They snuggled up on the couch, talking and laughing late into the night. It was a perfect ending to a perfect day.

In the days and weeks that followed, Emma and Liam shared the news with their friends and family. Everyone was thrilled for them, and they received countless messages of congratulations and well-wishes.

As they started planning their wedding, they kept coming back to the idea that their love was about more than just one big day. It was about all the little moments that made their relationship special. They decided to have a small, intimate ceremony with their closest friends and family, in a place that held meaning for them.

On their wedding day, as Emma walked down the aisle towards Liam, she felt a deep sense of gratitude. She was thankful for the love they shared, for the journey they had been on, and for the future that lay ahead.

When they said their vows, promising to love and support each other for the rest of their lives, Emma knew that they were not just words. They were a commitment to continue building a life together, full of love, joy, and unexpected moments.

As they exchanged rings and sealed their marriage with a kiss, the world seemed to fade away. It was just the two of them, standing together, ready to face whatever came their way.

And as they walked back down the aisle, hand in hand, Emma felt like the luckiest person in the world. She had found her soulmate, her best friend, and the love of her life. And she knew that together, they could conquer anything.

Erupted - To suddenly express strong emotions, such as cheering or applause.

- The coffee shop erupted in applause when Liam proposed to Emma, filling the air with joy and excitement.

Trembling - Shaking involuntarily, typically as a result of anxiety, excitement, or weakness.

- Emma's voice was trembling with emotion as she accepted Liam's marriage proposal in their favorite coffee shop.

Intertwined - Twisted or woven together; connected closely.

- Emma and Liam sat with their hands intertwined, symbolizing their deep connection and commitment to each other.

Raucous - Making or constituting a disturbingly harsh and loud noise.

- The raucous applause from the coffee shop customers added to the overwhelming emotion of Emma and Liam's engagement.

Thrilled - Extremely pleased and excited about something.

- Emma and Liam were thrilled to share the news of their

engagement with their friends and family.

Ceremony - A formal religious or public occasion, typically one celebrating a particular event or anniversary.

- Emma and Liam decided to have a small, intimate wedding ceremony with their closest friends and family.

Gratitude - The quality of being thankful; readiness to show appreciation for and to return kindness.

- Emma felt a deep sense of gratitude for the love she shared with Liam as she walked down the aisle on their wedding day.

Commitment - The state or quality of being dedicated to a cause, activity, or relationship.

- When Emma and Liam exchanged vows, they made a commitment to love and support each other for the rest of their lives.

Conquer - To successfully overcome a problem or obstacle.

- Emma believed that together with Liam, they could conquer any challenges that came their way in their married life.

Soulmate - A person ideally suited to another as a close friend or romantic partner.

- Emma felt like she had found her soulmate in Liam, knowing that they shared a deep connection and understanding.

36.

THE BUTTERFLY EFFECT

Sophie loved her morning walks through the park. It was her time to think and relax before starting her busy day. One sunny morning, as she walked along the path, she noticed an elderly woman struggling with her groceries. Without hesitation, Sophie approached her.

"Good morning," Sophie said with a smile. "Can I help you with those bags?"

The woman looked up, surprised but grateful. "Oh, thank you, dear. That would be wonderful. I'm on my way home, but these bags are heavier than I thought."

Sophie took two of the bags and walked with the woman. "I'm Sophie, by the way."

"I'm Mrs. Johnson," the woman replied. "Thank you so much for your help. My house is just a few blocks away."

As they walked, Mrs. Johnson shared stories about her life and her family. Sophie listened, enjoying the conversation. When they reached Mrs. Johnson's house, she invited Sophie in for a cup of tea as a thank you.

"I'd love to," Sophie said. They sat in the cozy kitchen, sipping tea and chatting. Sophie felt a sense of warmth and connection with Mrs. Johnson. She realized that this small act of kindness had made her morning much brighter.

Before leaving, Mrs. Johnson gave Sophie a small potted plant. "This is a thank you for your kindness," she said. "It's a butterfly plant. When it blooms, it attracts butterflies."

Sophie was touched. "Thank you, Mrs. Johnson. I'll take good care of it."

Over the next few weeks, Sophie noticed changes in her life. She felt happier and more connected to her community. She started volunteering at a local shelter, inspired by the feeling she had when helping Mrs. Johnson. She also made a point to perform small acts of kindness whenever she could, from holding doors open to helping neighbors with their chores.

One day, while volunteering at the shelter, Sophie met a young man named Alex. He was struggling to find a job and a place to live. Sophie remembered how good it felt to help Mrs. Johnson and decided to do what she could for Alex.

"Why don't you come to the community center tomorrow?" Sophie suggested. "They're holding a job fair. I can help you prepare your resume and practice for interviews."

Alex agreed, and the next day, Sophie helped him get ready. He felt more confident and hopeful. At the job fair, Alex met several employers and, by the end of the day, had two job offers. He was overjoyed and grateful for Sophie's help.

"Thank you, Sophie," Alex said. "You don't know how much this means to me."

Sophie smiled. "I'm happy to help, Alex. Just remember to pay it forward. Help someone else when you can."

A few months later, Sophie received an invitation to a community event organized by Alex. He had taken her advice to heart and wanted to give back. The event was a huge success, bringing together people from all walks of life to support each other and their community.

As Sophie looked around at the smiling faces, she felt a deep sense of fulfillment. Her small act of kindness towards Mrs. Johnson had set off a chain reaction, positively impacting many lives. She realized that even the smallest actions could have far-reaching consequences, much like the butterfly effect.

Reflecting on the journey, Sophie understood that kindness was a powerful force. It didn't take much to make a difference, but the impact could be profound. She felt grateful for the lesson and vowed to continue spreading kindness wherever she went.

Mrs. Johnson's butterfly plant had started to bloom, and Sophie noticed butterflies visiting her garden. Each time she saw them, she was reminded of the importance of kindness and the positive changes it could bring. She felt a sense of pride in knowing that her actions had contributed to a better, more connected community.

One afternoon, Sophie received a letter from Alex. He had started a nonprofit organization dedicated to helping people find jobs and housing. In the letter, he thanked her for her support and inspiration.

"Your kindness changed my life," he wrote. "I hope to do the same for others."

Sophie's heart swelled with pride and joy. She realized that the butterfly effect of her initial act of kindness had grown into something much bigger than she ever imagined. It had touched countless lives and created a ripple of positive change.

As she continued her morning walks through the park, Sophie made a point to look for opportunities to help others. She knew that even the smallest act of kindness could set off a chain reaction, making the world a better place, one person at a time.

Hesitation - Pausing before doing something, often because of uncertainty or reluctance.

- Sophie approached Mrs. Johnson without hesitation, offering to help her with the heavy bags.

Volunteering - Offering to do work or provide a service willingly and without payment.

- Inspired by her experience with Mrs. Johnson, Sophie started volunteering at a local shelter to help those in need.

Confident - Feeling sure about your own abilities or qualities.

- After preparing for interviews with Sophie's help, Alex felt more confident about his job prospects.

Overjoyed - Extremely happy or delighted.

- Alex was overjoyed when he received two job offers at the job fair, thanks to Sophie's assistance.

Fulfillment - The feeling of satisfaction or happiness as a result of fully developing one's abilities or character.

- Sophie felt a deep sense of fulfillment as she saw the positive impact of her kindness on the community.

Invitation - A written or verbal request inviting someone to go somewhere or to do something.

- Sophie received an invitation from Alex to attend a community event he organized to give back to others.

Inspiration - Something or someone that gives you new ideas and the desire to create or do something.

- Alex started a nonprofit organization inspired by Sophie's kindness and support.

Pride - A feeling of deep pleasure or satisfaction derived from one's own achievements, qualities, or possessions.

- Sophie felt pride and joy as she read Alex's letter, realizing the positive impact of her initial act of kindness.

Grateful - Feeling or showing an appreciation of kindness; thankful.

- Alex was grateful to Sophie for helping him find job opportunities and for inspiring him to start a nonprofit organization.

Ripple - A small wave or series of waves on the surface of water, caused by a slight breeze or an object dropping into it; used metaphorically here to describe a spreading effect or series of consequences.

- Sophie's act of kindness created a ripple of positive change that touched many lives in the community.

37.

THE TIME CAPSULE

One sunny Saturday afternoon, four friends, Emma, Ryan, Olivia, and Jake, decided to meet at their old elementary school playground. They hadn't seen each other in years and thought it would be fun to reminisce about their childhood. As they walked around the playground, memories started flooding back.

"Do you remember when we used to play hide and seek here?" Emma asked, smiling.

"Of course," Ryan replied. "And the time Jake got stuck in the tree?"

Jake laughed. "Yeah, I remember. I thought I was never going to get down!"

As they continued to walk and talk, Olivia suddenly stopped. "Wait a minute," she said. "Do you guys remember the time capsule we buried in the schoolyard?"

Everyone stopped and looked at her, surprised. "Oh wow, I totally forgot about that!" Emma exclaimed. "We buried it in fifth grade, didn't we?"

"Yes," Olivia confirmed. "We buried it under that big oak tree near the baseball field."

"Let's go find it!" Ryan suggested, excitement in his voice.

The group eagerly made their way to the oak tree. After a bit of digging, they hit something solid. "I think this is it!" Jake said, carefully pulling out a small, rusty metal box.

They sat down in a circle around the box, and Ryan slowly opened it. Inside, they found a collection of items they had placed there years ago: letters, toys, pictures, and other small treasures.

Emma picked up a letter and began to read it aloud. "Dear future me, I hope you are doing well. I want to be a veterinarian when I grow up. Are you a vet yet? Love, Emma."

Emma smiled and looked at her friends. "Well, I'm not a vet, but I do work with animals at a shelter. It's funny to see what I dreamed of back then."

Ryan picked up another letter. "Dear Ryan, I hope you are still friends with everyone. Remember to always have fun and be happy. Sincerely, Ryan."

"Good advice," Ryan said, laughing. "And yes, I'm still friends with you all, so I guess I did something right."

Olivia found a small toy car and laughed. "This was my favorite toy! I can't believe I put it in here."

Jake found a picture of the four of them at a school play. "Look at us! We were so young."

As they continued to explore the contents of the time capsule, they shared stories and laughed about their childhood memories. They realized how much they had changed and grown since those days.

"Finding this time capsule was a great idea," Jake said. "It's amazing to see how far we've come."

"Yeah, and it's nice to remember our childhood," Olivia added. "We had so much fun back then."

Emma nodded. "It's important to remember where we came from and the dreams we had. Even if our lives didn't turn out exactly as we planned, we're all doing well."

Ryan looked around at his friends. "I think we should bury another time capsule. It would be fun to look back on our lives in another ten years."

Everyone agreed. They found a new box and each wrote a letter to their future selves. They included some small items that were meaningful to them now.

"Dear future Emma," Emma wrote. "I hope you are still working with animals and making a difference in their lives. Remember to always follow your passion."

"Dear future Ryan," Ryan wrote. "I hope you are happy and healthy. Keep having fun and stay close to your friends."

"Dear future Olivia," Olivia wrote. "I hope you are still creative and doing something you love. Remember to always find joy in the little things."

"Dear future Jake," Jake wrote. "I hope you are successful and happy. Keep being adventurous and trying new things."

They placed their letters and items in the new time capsule and buried it under the oak tree. They promised to meet again in ten years to dig it up.

As they walked away from the playground, they felt a sense of nostalgia and gratitude for their friendship and shared memories. They knew that no matter where life took them, they would always have these moments to look back on.

"This was a great day," Emma said. "I'm so glad we did this."

"Me too," Ryan agreed. "Let's not wait so long to get together next time."

Olivia and Jake nodded in agreement. "Definitely," Olivia said. "We need to make more memories together."

As they parted ways, each friend felt a renewed sense of connection and appreciation for the past and excitement for the future. They knew that their friendship was something special and that they would always be there for each other, no matter what.

Reminisce - To indulge in enjoyable recollection of past events.

- As they walked around the playground, memories started flooding back, and they began to reminisce about their childhood adventures.

Eagerly - With great enthusiasm or desire.

- The group eagerly made their way to the oak tree to uncover the buried time capsule from their school days.

Meaningful - Having significance; conveying a deep or important message.

- They included some small items in the time capsule that were meaningful to them at that moment in their lives.

Nostalgia - A sentimental longing or wistful affection for the past, typically for a period or place with happy personal associations.

- As they walked away from the playground, they felt a sense of nostalgia for their childhood and the carefree days spent there.

Gratitude - The quality of being thankful; readiness to show appreciation for and to return kindness.

- They felt gratitude for their friendship and shared memories as they buried the new time capsule under the oak tree.

Renewed - Restored to a better, more vigorous, or more effective state.

- Each friend felt a renewed sense of connection and

appreciation for their friendship after digging up the old time capsule.

Appreciation - Recognition and enjoyment of the good qualities of someone or something.

- They parted ways with a renewed sense of connection and appreciation for their shared experiences and friendship.

Promise - A declaration or assurance that one will do a particular thing or that guarantees that a particular thing will happen.

- They promised to meet again in ten years to dig up the new time capsule they buried under the oak tree.

Excitement - A feeling of great enthusiasm and eagerness.

- There was excitement in Ryan's voice as he suggested burying another time capsule to look back on in the future.

Adventure - An unusual and exciting or daring experience.

- Jake wrote in his letter to his future self to keep being adventurous and trying new things.

38.

THE BEST DAY EVER

Tommy woke up early on Saturday morning, feeling excited. It was going to be the best day ever, and he could hardly wait. His family had planned a special day out, and Tommy had been looking forward to it all week.

He jumped out of bed and ran to the kitchen, where his mom was making breakfast. "Good morning, Mom!" he said cheerfully. "Is it time to go yet?"

"Good morning, Tommy," his mom replied with a smile. "Not yet, but soon. First, you need to eat your breakfast."

Tommy quickly ate his pancakes and drank his orange juice. His dad came into the kitchen, carrying a picnic basket. "Are you ready for our adventure, Tommy?" he asked.

"Yes, I am!" Tommy said, his eyes shining with excitement.

After breakfast, Tommy's family got into the car and drove to the zoo. It was Tommy's favorite place because he loved animals. When they arrived, Tommy could barely contain his excitement.

"Let's start with the lions!" he suggested.

They walked to the lion enclosure, and Tommy watched in awe as the big cats roamed around. "Look at their manes, Dad!" he said. "They're so majestic."

"They are," his dad agreed. "Lions are known as the kings of the jungle."

Next, they visited the elephant area. Tommy was amazed by

the size of the elephants and how they used their trunks to pick up food. "Can you believe how big they are, Mom?" he asked.

"They're enormous," his mom said. "And very intelligent, too."

Tommy's family spent the whole morning at the zoo, visiting different animals and learning about them. They saw giraffes, zebras, monkeys, and even a polar bear. Each animal was fascinating in its own way, and Tommy loved every minute of it.

Around lunchtime, they found a shady spot in the zoo and sat down to have their picnic. Tommy's mom had packed sandwiches, fruit, and cookies. They ate together, laughing and talking about the animals they had seen.

"This is the best picnic ever," Tommy said, taking a bite of his sandwich.

After lunch, they went to the zoo's playground. Tommy climbed the jungle gym, slid down the slides, and played on the swings. His parents watched him with smiles on their faces.

"You really are having the best day ever, aren't you, Tommy?" his dad asked.

"Yes, I am!" Tommy shouted from the top of the jungle gym. "This is the best day of my life!"

In the afternoon, they visited the zoo's aquarium. Tommy loved watching the colorful fish swim around. He pressed his face against the glass, mesmerized by the underwater world.

"Look at the clownfish, Mom!" he said, pointing to a bright orange fish. "Just like in the movie!"

"They're beautiful, aren't they?" his mom said.

They also saw jellyfish, seahorses, and even a big shark. Tommy was fascinated by the way the shark moved through the water.

As the day went on, Tommy felt like he was on a grand adventure. They rode the zoo train, which took them on a tour around the entire zoo. Tommy waved at the animals as they passed by and laughed with joy.

By the time they left the zoo, the sun was starting to set. Tommy was tired but very happy. "Thank you for the best day ever," he said to his parents as they walked back to the car.

"We're glad you had fun, Tommy," his mom said, giving him a hug.

On the way home, they stopped for ice cream. Tommy chose chocolate, his favorite flavor. They sat together at a picnic table, enjoying their treats.

"This day just keeps getting better and better," Tommy said between bites of ice cream.

When they finally got home, Tommy was exhausted but happy. He took a quick bath and got ready for bed. As his mom tucked him in, he smiled up at her.

"Today was amazing, Mom," he said. "I wish every day could be like this."

"Me too, Tommy," his mom replied. "But that's what makes days like today so special. We get to create wonderful memories together."

"Good night, Mom," Tommy said, closing his eyes.

"Good night, Tommy," his mom whispered. "Sweet dreams."

As Tommy drifted off to sleep, he thought about all the fun he had that day. He dreamed of lions, elephants, and colorful fish. It had truly been the best day ever, and he knew he would remember it forever.

Excitement - A feeling of eager enthusiasm and interest.

- Tommy woke up early, feeling excitement about the special day his family had planned at the zoo.

Adventure - An exciting or unusual experience; a bold, usually risky undertaking.

- Tommy felt like he was on a grand adventure as he explored the zoo and saw all the different animals.

Fascinated - Extremely interested in something and paying close attention to it.

- Tommy was fascinated by the colorful fish swimming in the aquarium, especially the clownfish that reminded him of a movie.

Picnic - An occasion when a packed meal is eaten outdoors, especially during an outing to a park or a zoo.

- Tommy's family enjoyed a picnic lunch at the zoo, sitting together and discussing the animals they had seen.

Mesmerized - Captivated or fascinated to the point of losing awareness of one's surroundings.

- Tommy pressed his face against the aquarium glass, mesmerized by the graceful movement of the shark.

Joy - A feeling of great happiness and delight.

- Tommy laughed with joy as he rode the zoo train and waved at the animals along the way.

Memories - Things remembered from the past; recollections.

- Tommy knew he would cherish the memories of his best day ever at the zoo for a long time.

Tired but happy - Feeling physically exhausted yet content and pleased with how things have gone.

- By the end of the day, Tommy was tired but happy after a day full of excitement and adventure at the zoo.

Special - Better, greater, or otherwise different from what is usual.

- Tommy's mom explained that days like today are special because they create wonderful memories together as a family.

Create - To cause something to happen as a result of one's actions.

- Tommy and his family created wonderful memories together during their best day ever at the zoo.

39.

THE SECRET INGREDIENT

Sophia had always loved cooking. Ever since she was a little girl, she had spent countless hours in the kitchen with her grandmother, learning the secrets of delicious meals. Now, as a grown woman, she was a chef at a popular restaurant in the city. However, she felt like something was missing. Her dishes were good, but she wanted them to be great.

One evening, after a long day at the restaurant, Sophia was browsing through an old cookbook she found in her grandmother's attic. The cookbook was worn and covered in dust, but it was full of fascinating recipes. As she turned the pages, one recipe caught her eye: "Grandma's Secret Ingredient Soup."

Curious, Sophia read through the ingredients. Most of them were familiar, but there was one she had never seen before: "Loveberry." There was no explanation or description of this mysterious ingredient. Intrigued, Sophia decided to visit the local market the next day to see if anyone knew about this "Loveberry."

The next morning, she arrived at the bustling market. She went from stall to stall, asking the vendors if they had ever heard of Loveberry. Most of them just shook their heads or gave her puzzled looks. She was about to give up when she saw an old man sitting at a small, dusty stall at the far end of the market. His stall was filled with strange and exotic herbs and spices.

"Excuse me, sir," Sophia said politely. "Do you know what a Loveberry is?"

The old man looked up and smiled. "Ah, the Loveberry," he said in a soft, raspy voice. "Not many people ask about that. It is a rare and special ingredient."

Sophia's eyes lit up. "Do you have any? I would love to buy some."

The old man reached under his stall and pulled out a small, wooden box. He opened it carefully, revealing a handful of bright red berries. They looked like tiny rubies. "These are Loveberries," he said. "But they are not just any berries. They must be used with care and respect."

Sophia bought a small bag of Loveberries and hurried back to her kitchen. She couldn't wait to try them out. She decided to make a simple soup, similar to the one in her grandmother's cookbook, but she added a few Loveberries to the mix. As the soup simmered, a wonderful aroma filled the kitchen. It smelled better than anything she had ever cooked before.

When the soup was ready, Sophia tasted it. The flavor was incredible. It was rich and savory, with a hint of sweetness that she had never experienced before. The Loveberries had transformed her simple soup into something magical.

Excited, Sophia decided to serve the soup as a special dish at the restaurant that night. The customers were amazed. They couldn't stop talking about how delicious the soup was. Word spread quickly, and soon people were coming from all over the city to taste Sophia's special soup.

One evening, a well-known food critic came to the restaurant. Sophia was nervous but hopeful. She served him a bowl of her Loveberry soup, and he tasted it thoughtfully. After a few moments, he smiled and asked to speak with her.

"This is one of the best soups I have ever tasted," he said. "What is your secret?"

Sophia hesitated for a moment but decided to be honest. "It's an old family recipe," she said. "The secret ingredient is something called a Loveberry."

The food critic raised his eyebrows. "A Loveberry, you say? I have heard of them, but they are very rare. You have truly created something special here."

The next day, the food critic's review was published. He praised Sophia's soup, calling it a masterpiece. The restaurant became even more popular, and Sophia's career took off. She was invited to cook on television shows, write a cookbook, and even open her own restaurant.

Throughout all of this, Sophia never forgot the old man at the market. She visited him often, buying more Loveberries and learning more about their unique qualities. She also shared her success with him, grateful for his help in discovering the secret ingredient that changed her life.

Sophia's new restaurant, "Loveberry Delights," became a huge success. People came from far and wide to taste her dishes, each one infused with the magic of Loveberries. Sophia continued to experiment with different recipes, always finding new ways to use the special ingredient.

One day, as she was preparing for the evening's service, she thought about her grandmother and the many hours they had spent together in the kitchen. She smiled, knowing that her grandmother would be proud of her. The Loveberries had not only transformed her career but had also brought her closer to her roots and the memories she cherished.

As she looked around her bustling restaurant, filled with happy customers, Sophia felt a deep sense of gratitude. She had found the secret ingredient, not just in her cooking, but in her life. It was passion, love, and the joy of sharing her creations with others. And that, she realized, was the true magic of the Loveberry.

Chef - A professional cook who is in charge of a kitchen or a restaurant.

- Sophia worked hard to become a chef at a popular restaurant in the city.

Mysterious - Difficult or impossible to understand, explain, or identify.

- Sophia was intrigued by the mysterious ingredient called Loveberry in her grandmother's old cookbook.

Exotic - Unusual and interesting because it comes from or is related to a distant foreign country.

- The old man at the market sold exotic herbs and spices that Sophia had never seen before.

Aroma - A pleasant and distinctive smell, especially one that is pleasant.

- The Loveberry soup filled Sophia's kitchen with a wonderful aroma that made her mouth water.

Incredible - Extremely good; amazing.

- The flavor of the soup made with Loveberries was incredible, and Sophia knew she had created something special.

Magical - Beautiful or delightful in a way that seems removed from everyday life; enchanting.

- The addition of Loveberries turned Sophia's simple soup into something magical that everyone loved.

Masterpiece - A work of outstanding artistry, skill, or

workmanship.

- The food critic described Sophia's Loveberry soup as a masterpiece, praising its unique flavor and creativity.

Grateful - Feeling or showing an appreciation of kindness; thankful.

- Sophia was grateful to the old man at the market for introducing her to the rare Loveberries that transformed her cooking.

Passion - Strong and barely controllable emotion; intense enthusiasm for something.

- Sophia's passion for cooking and experimenting with new ingredients led her to discover the secret of the Loveberry.

Roots - The origins or sources of something; the basic cause, source, or origin of something.

- Sophia felt closer to her roots and cherished memories of cooking with her grandmother while using the Loveberries in her dishes.

40.

THE LANGUAGE OF FLOWERS

Anna had always loved flowers. As a child, she spent hours in her grandmother's garden, learning the names and meanings of each blossom. Now, as an adult, she owned a small flower shop in the heart of the city. "Bloom & Blossom" was known for its beautiful arrangements and the special touch Anna added to every bouquet.

One sunny morning, as Anna was arranging a fresh delivery of roses, lilies, and daisies, a young man entered the shop. He looked nervous and unsure, glancing around at the various flowers.

"Hello," Anna greeted him with a warm smile. "How can I help you today?"

"Hi," the young man replied, shifting from foot to foot. "I need to buy some flowers, but I'm not sure what to get. They're for someone special."

Anna's eyes twinkled. She loved helping customers choose the perfect flowers. "Well, let's start with what message you want to send. Flowers can say a lot without words."

The young man looked thoughtful. "I want to tell her that I care about her and that I'm sorry for a mistake I made."

Anna nodded. "How about a combination of white roses and purple hyacinths? White roses symbolize purity and new beginnings, while purple hyacinths represent apologies and deep regret."

The young man's face lit up. "That sounds perfect. Thank you."

Anna carefully arranged the flowers, adding a touch of greenery for balance. As she handed the bouquet to the young man, he smiled gratefully. "I hope she likes them."

"I'm sure she will," Anna replied. "Good luck!"

As the young man left the shop, Anna felt a sense of satisfaction. She loved knowing that her flowers helped people express their feelings.

Later that afternoon, an older woman entered the shop, looking around with a sad expression. Anna approached her gently. "Hello, is there something I can help you with?"

The woman sighed. "I'm looking for flowers to take to a friend's funeral. I want them to show respect and love."

Anna thought for a moment. "Lilies are a classic choice for funerals. They symbolize the restored innocence of the soul. You could also add some white chrysanthemums, which represent loyalty and devoted love."

The woman nodded slowly. "That sounds right. Thank you."

Anna put together a beautiful arrangement of lilies and chrysanthemums, tying them with a soft, white ribbon. The woman looked at the bouquet with teary eyes. "These are perfect. Thank you so much."

As the woman left, Anna's heart ached for her loss but also felt warm knowing she had helped in a small way.

The next day, a young girl came into the shop, clutching a crumpled piece of paper. She looked around, wide-eyed, and approached Anna shyly. "Hi, I'm supposed to get flowers for my mom's birthday, but I don't know which ones."

Anna knelt down to the girl's level, smiling kindly. "That's very sweet of you. Do you know what kind of flowers your mom likes?"

The girl shook her head. "No, but she likes bright colors."

"Okay," Anna said, thinking. "How about a mix of sunflowers and tulips? Sunflowers are bright and cheerful, and tulips come in many beautiful colors. They both symbolize happiness and love."

The girl's face lit up. "Yes, that sounds great!"

Anna selected the freshest sunflowers and colorful tulips, arranging them in a small, charming bouquet. The girl handed over her carefully saved money and took the flowers with a big smile. "Thank you!"

"You're welcome," Anna replied, watching the girl skip out of the shop.

As the days passed, Anna helped many more customers, each with their unique stories and emotions. A young couple came in looking for flowers to celebrate their anniversary, and Anna suggested red roses for love and white lilies for commitment. A man bought daisies and forget-me-nots for his sister, who was moving away, to symbolize hope and remembrance.

One afternoon, Anna received a visit from Mrs. Johnson, a regular customer who often bought flowers for her garden. Today, however, Mrs. Johnson seemed more contemplative than usual.

"Anna, dear," she began, "I have a question. What flowers would you recommend for forgiveness?"

Anna smiled softly. "For forgiveness, you might consider white tulips. They represent new beginnings and apologies. You could also add blue hyacinths, which symbolize deep regret."

Mrs. Johnson nodded thoughtfully. "Thank you, Anna. I have some mending to do with an old friend."

As Anna prepared the arrangement, she couldn't help but feel a deep connection to her customers. Each bouquet she crafted was a message of love, sorrow, joy, or hope. Flowers were her way of helping people communicate their deepest feelings.

One evening, as Anna was closing up the shop, she found a small note left on the counter. It read, "Thank you for helping me express what words couldn't. Your flowers made a difference." The note was unsigned, but it filled Anna with a warm glow.

She realized that her flower shop was more than just a business. It was a place where emotions bloomed and where the language of flowers spoke the words of the heart. Anna felt grateful for her role in this beautiful exchange and looked forward to continuing her work, one blossom at a time.

Blossom - To develop or mature in a promising or healthy way; to flourish.

- Anna's flower shop, "Bloom & Blossom," was known for its beautiful arrangements.

Satisfaction - The fulfillment of one's wishes, expectations, or needs, or the pleasure derived from this.

- Anna felt a sense of satisfaction knowing her flowers helped people express their feelings.

Gently - In a mild or kindly manner.

- Anna approached the older woman gently, sensing her sadness about choosing flowers for a funeral.

Cheerful - Noticeably happy and optimistic.

- The young girl wanted bright and cheerful flowers for her mom's birthday bouquet.

Contemplative - Involving prolonged thought; reflective.

- Mrs. Johnson seemed contemplative as she asked Anna for flower recommendations for forgiveness.

Crafted - To make or manufacture (something) with skill and careful attention to detail.

- Anna crafted each bouquet with care, ensuring it conveyed the right message for her customers.

Anonymous - (of a person) not identified by name; of unknown name.

- Anna received an anonymous note thanking her for helping express emotions through flowers.

Grateful - Feeling or showing an appreciation of kindness; thankful.

- Anna felt grateful for her role in helping customers communicate their deepest feelings through flowers.

Connection - A relationship in which a person, thing, or idea is linked or associated with something else.

- Anna felt a deep connection to her customers as she helped them choose flowers for various occasions.

Exchange - The act of giving or taking one thing in return for another; a trade.

- Anna saw her flower shop as a place where emotions bloomed and the exchange of heartfelt messages occurred.

41.

THE ROAD TRIP

"Are you sure this is a good idea?" asked Mark, looking at the old map spread out on the hood of his car. The map had been in his family for years and showed a scenic route through the countryside.

"Absolutely," replied Sarah, his best friend since high school. "We need a break, and what better way to relax than a road trip?"

"It's going to be amazing," added Jake, their other friend, who was busy packing snacks into a cooler. "Just imagine the open road, great music, and us having fun."

The three friends had decided to take a road trip to clear their minds and escape their daily routines. They had all been feeling stressed from work and needed an adventure.

"Alright, let's do this," said Mark, folding the map and placing it in the car. He slid into the driver's seat, while Sarah took the front passenger seat and Jake climbed into the back.

As they drove out of the city, the noise and stress began to fade away. The road ahead was long and winding, but it was also full of possibilities. The first few hours were filled with laughter, singing along to their favorite songs, and joking about old times.

"Remember that time in high school when you tried to impress Lisa by doing that skateboard trick?" Sarah teased Mark.

"How could I forget? I ended up in the hospital with a broken arm," Mark laughed.

They stopped at a small diner for lunch, where the friendly waitress served them the best burgers and fries they had ever tasted. The walls of the diner were decorated with pictures of the local area, showing beautiful landscapes and historical landmarks.

"This place is so charming," Sarah said, taking a sip of her milkshake. "I feel like we're in a different world."

"That's the beauty of road trips," Jake replied. "You discover places you never knew existed."

After lunch, they continued their journey. The scenery changed from city skyscrapers to rolling hills and vast fields of wildflowers. They passed through small towns where people waved at them as they drove by.

"Let's stop here for a bit," Sarah suggested when they reached a picturesque lake surrounded by trees. They parked the car and got out, stretching their legs and taking in the fresh air.

"This is perfect," Mark said, sitting on a large rock by the water. "We should come here more often."

"Agreed," Jake said, tossing a stone into the lake and watching it skip across the water. "It's so peaceful."

As the sun began to set, they decided to find a place to stay for the night. They came across a cozy bed-and-breakfast run by an elderly couple. The couple welcomed them warmly and showed them to their rooms.

"This place is lovely," Sarah said, admiring the antique furniture and the floral wallpaper.

The next morning, after a hearty breakfast, they continued their journey. They visited a nearby national park, where they hiked through the woods and saw breathtaking waterfalls.

"I can't believe how beautiful this place is," Jake said, snapping pictures with his camera. "These memories will last forever."

Their road trip took unexpected turns, like when they had to stop to help a farmer with a flat tire on his tractor. In return, the farmer invited them to his farmhouse for a homemade dinner.

"This is the best pie I've ever had," Mark said, enjoying a slice of apple pie made by the farmer's wife.

As the days went by, their adventure became even more memorable. They encountered a music festival in a small town, where they danced to live bands under the stars. They found a hidden beach where they swam and built sandcastles like they were kids again.

One evening, as they sat around a campfire they had built by a remote campsite, they talked about their lives and their future dreams.

"This trip has been exactly what I needed," Sarah said, staring into the flames. "I feel so much lighter."

"Same here," Mark agreed. "I realize now how important it is to take a break and appreciate the simple things."

Jake nodded. "It's funny how we get so caught up in our routines that we forget to live. This trip has reminded me to enjoy the journey, not just the destination."

Their road trip was coming to an end, but the memories they made would stay with them forever. As they drove back to the city, they promised to take more trips together and to never forget the lessons they had learned on the open road.

"Let's make this a tradition," Sarah suggested. "An annual road trip to explore new places and reconnect."

"Absolutely," Mark said, smiling. "We still have so many places to see."

Jake raised his drink. "To more adventures and unforgettable memories."

They all clinked their drinks together, feeling grateful for the journey they had shared. The road trip had brought them closer, filled them with new energy, and taught them to cherish every moment.

Escape - To break free from confinement or control; to leave behind or get away from something undesirable.

- The friends decided to take a road trip to escape their daily routines and relax.

Adventure - An exciting or unusual experience; a bold, usually risky undertaking with an uncertain outcome.

- Driving through unknown countryside, exploring small towns, and hiking in national parks made their road trip an unforgettable adventure.

Charming - Pleasant or attractive; full of charm.

- Sarah described the small diner they visited as charming, with its local decor and friendly atmosphere.

Picturesque - Visually attractive, especially in a quaint or pretty style.

- They stopped by a picturesque lake surrounded by trees, where they enjoyed the peaceful scenery.

Cozy - Giving a feeling of comfort, warmth, and relaxation.

- The bed-and-breakfast they stayed at was cozy, with its antique furniture and floral wallpaper.

Breathtaking - Extremely impressive or beautiful in a way that takes one's breath away.

- The national park they visited had breathtaking

waterfalls and scenic hiking trails.

Memorable - Worth remembering or easily remembered, especially because of being special or unusual.

- The unexpected encounters, like helping a farmer and enjoying homemade pie, made their road trip even more memorable.

Remote - Far away from other places, buildings, or people; secluded.

- They built a campfire in a remote campsite, surrounded by nature and under a starry sky.

Tradition - A belief, custom, or way of doing something that has existed for a long time among a particular group of people.

- Sarah suggested making their annual road trip a tradition, to explore new places and strengthen their friendship.

Grateful - Feeling or showing thanks; thankful.

- They were grateful for the lessons learned on their road trip — to appreciate life's simple joys and enjoy the journey itself.

42.

THE POWER
OF MUSIC

Mrs. Thompson was the music teacher at Evergreen High School. She had been teaching there for over ten years and had seen many students come and go. Her love for music was clear in everything she did, from the way she played the piano to how she conducted the school choir.

One day, a new student named Emily joined her class. Emily was shy and quiet, always sitting in the back of the room. Mrs. Thompson noticed that Emily never participated in class discussions and rarely smiled. She wondered what was troubling her.

"Emily, could you stay for a few minutes after class?" Mrs. Thompson asked one day. Emily looked surprised but nodded.

After the other students left, Mrs. Thompson sat down next to Emily. "I've noticed you're very quiet in class. Is everything okay?"

Emily looked down at her hands. "I'm fine," she said softly.

Mrs. Thompson wasn't convinced. "You know, music can be a great way to express how we feel. Have you ever thought about learning to play an instrument or joining the choir?"

Emily shrugged. "I don't think I'm good at music."

Mrs. Thompson smiled warmly. "Everyone has music inside them. Sometimes we just need to find the right way to let it out. How about you try playing the piano with me after school? Just once, and if you don't like it, we can find something else you might enjoy."

Emily hesitated but finally agreed. "Okay, I'll try."

The next day, Emily stayed after school. Mrs. Thompson showed her a simple melody on the piano. Emily watched closely and then tried to play it. At first, she made a few mistakes, but Mrs. Thompson was patient and encouraging.

"That was great for a first try, Emily! Let's do it again, slowly."

Emily practiced every day after school with Mrs. Thompson. Slowly but surely, she began to improve. She started to enjoy playing the piano and even smiled a little more each day.

One afternoon, as they were practicing, Emily said, "Mrs. Thompson, can I ask you something?"

"Of course, Emily. What's on your mind?"

"Why did you become a music teacher?"

Mrs. Thompson thought for a moment. "I've always loved music. When I was your age, I had a wonderful music teacher who inspired me. She showed me how powerful music can be. It can bring joy, comfort, and even help us through tough times. I wanted to share that with others."

Emily nodded. "I think I understand now. Music makes me feel better. It helps me forget about my problems for a while."

Mrs. Thompson smiled. "I'm glad to hear that, Emily. Music has a way of touching our hearts and souls. That's why it's so special."

As the weeks went by, Emily became more confident. She started participating in class and even joined the school choir. Mrs. Thompson noticed a big change in her. Emily was no longer the quiet, shy girl who sat in the back of the room. She was now an active and happy member of the music class.

One day, Mrs. Thompson announced that the school was going to hold a music concert. "I would like each of you to perform something special," she said. "It can be a song, an instrument, or even a dance."

Emily felt a little nervous but also excited. She decided to play the piano piece she had been practicing. On the day of the concert, the auditorium was filled with students, teachers, and parents. Emily's heart was pounding as she walked onto the stage.

Mrs. Thompson gave her an encouraging nod from the audience. Emily took a deep breath and began to play. As her fingers moved across the keys, she felt a sense of calm wash over her. She was no longer nervous. She was doing something she loved, and it felt amazing.

When she finished, the audience erupted in applause. Emily looked out and saw her parents, beaming with pride. Mrs. Thompson was clapping the loudest of all.

After the concert, Mrs. Thompson hugged Emily. "You were wonderful, Emily. I'm so proud of you."

"Thank you, Mrs. Thompson," Emily said, her eyes shining with happiness. "I couldn't have done it without you."

Mrs. Thompson smiled. "Remember, Emily, the power of music is inside you. It will always be there to lift you up and help you through any challenges you face."

Emily nodded. "I'll never forget that."

From that day on, Emily continued to grow in confidence and skill. She joined more music classes and even started teaching younger students how to play the piano. She had found her passion, and it all began with the encouragement of a kind and caring music teacher.

Years later, when Emily graduated from high school, she decided to become a music teacher herself. She wanted to inspire others, just as Mrs. Thompson had inspired her. She knew that the power of music could change lives, and she was determined to share that gift with the world.

Express - To convey (a thought or feeling) in words, actions, or through artistic creation.

- Mrs. Thompson encouraged Emily to use music as a way to express her emotions and thoughts.

Encourage - To give support, confidence, or hope to someone; to motivate.

- Mrs. Thompson's encouragement helped Emily gain confidence in playing the piano.

Inspire - To fill someone with the urge or ability to do or feel something, especially to do something creative.

- Emily was inspired by Mrs. Thompson's passion for music to pursue her own musical journey.

Participant - A person who takes part or is involved in an activity.

- Emily went from being a quiet observer to an active participant in the school choir.

Confident - Feeling or showing certainty about one's ability or quality.

- With Mrs. Thompson's guidance, Emily became more confident in her musical abilities.

Concert - A public performance of music or dance, usually given by one or more performers.

- Emily felt nervous before her piano performance at the

school concert, but she did well.

Erupt - To break out suddenly and dramatically, especially into applause or laughter.

- After Emily finished her piano piece, the audience erupted in enthusiastic applause.

Pride - A feeling of deep pleasure or satisfaction derived from one's own achievements, the achievements of those with whom one is closely associated, or from qualities or possessions that are widely admired.

- Emily's parents watched her performance at the concert with pride.

Passion - Strong and barely controllable emotion; a strong liking or desire for something.

- Emily found her passion for music through Mrs. Thompson's guidance and support.

Determined - Having made a firm decision and being resolved not to change it; strongly motivated to achieve a goal.

- Emily was determined to become a music teacher and inspire others, just as Mrs. Thompson had inspired her.

43.

THE RAINY DAY

It was a typical morning in the small town of Maplewood. The sky was overcast, and a gentle drizzle was falling. Most people were indoors, avoiding the wet weather. It had been raining for several days, and the townspeople were starting to feel a bit gloomy.

At the town's bakery, Mr. Jenkins was preparing his famous bread. He looked out the window and sighed. "Another rainy day," he said to himself. "I hope it doesn't keep people away."

As the morning progressed, the rain began to fall harder. The streets were empty, except for a few cars driving slowly through the puddles. In her cozy home, Mrs. Parker was knitting a sweater for her grandson. She glanced at the rain and thought about how much she missed the sun.

Across town, in a small café, Emily was serving hot coffee to the few customers who had braved the weather. "This rain is never-ending," she said to her coworker, Jake. "I hope it stops soon."

Jake nodded. "Yeah, but you know what? Sometimes, rainy days can bring unexpected surprises."

Emily looked at him curiously. "What do you mean?"

"You'll see," Jake replied with a smile.

Just then, the door opened, and a man walked in, shaking the water off his umbrella. He looked around and spotted an empty table near the window. As he sat down, Emily brought him a menu.

"Good morning," she said. "What can I get for you today?"

The man smiled. "Just a coffee, please. And maybe a slice of that delicious-looking apple pie."

"Coming right up," Emily replied. She noticed that despite the rain, the man seemed cheerful.

As she served his coffee and pie, the man looked out the window. "You know," he said, "I've always loved rainy days. They remind me to slow down and appreciate the little things."

Emily smiled. "That's a nice way to look at it."

The man nodded. "When I was a child, my mother used to say that rainy days were perfect for baking cookies, reading books, and spending time with family."

Emily thought about her own childhood. "My mom used to make hot chocolate and we'd play board games," she said. "Those were some of the best days."

As the morning went on, more people started to venture out. They came into the café, shaking off their umbrellas and sharing stories of their rainy day activities. Some had been baking, others had been watching movies or playing games with their children. The café filled with the warm scent of coffee and the sound of laughter.

Meanwhile, in the town square, a group of children were splashing in the puddles, their laughter echoing through the streets. Mrs. Parker, who had finished her knitting, watched them from her window. She smiled and remembered how much fun she used to have playing in the rain as a child.

Feeling inspired, she decided to bake a batch of cookies. As the cookies baked, the sweet aroma filled her home. She thought about how a simple rainy day could bring so much joy.

Back at the bakery, Mr. Jenkins had a similar idea. He started baking extra treats, hoping to brighten someone's day. As people came in to buy bread, he offered them free cookies. "A little something to make this rainy day better," he said with a wink.

The townspeople were delighted. They took their cookies and thanked Mr. Jenkins, feeling a little warmer and happier despite the rain. Word spread quickly, and soon the bakery was filled with people, all sharing stories and enjoying the unexpected treat.

At the café, Emily noticed that the mood had changed. People were smiling and chatting, and the rain outside didn't seem so bad anymore. She thought about what Jake had said earlier. Maybe rainy days really did bring unexpected surprises.

As the day went on, the rain began to lighten. People started to leave the café, their spirits lifted. Emily and Jake cleaned up, feeling satisfied with a job well done.

Before leaving, the cheerful man who had come in earlier approached Emily. "Thank you for the coffee and pie," he said. "And for reminding me of the simple joys in life."

Emily smiled. "Thank you for sharing your perspective. It really did make this rainy day special."

As the man left, Emily looked out the window. The rain had almost stopped, and a faint rainbow was starting to appear in the sky. She felt a sense of contentment, knowing that even a rainy day could bring so much joy and connection.

In the end, the small town of Maplewood had experienced a rainy day like no other. The simple acts of kindness, the shared stories, and the unexpected moments of joy had turned a gloomy day into something memorable. And as the townspeople went to bed that night, they felt grateful for the rain and the happiness it had brought into their lives.

Gloomy - Dark, dim, or dull, especially in an atmospheric way; causing or feeling sadness.

- The townspeople were feeling gloomy after several days of continuous rain.

Knitting - Creating fabric by interlocking loops of yarn with needles.

- Mrs. Parker enjoyed spending rainy days indoors, knitting sweaters for her family.

Brave - Showing courage or willingness to face difficulty, danger, or pain.

- Despite the heavy rain, a few brave customers ventured out to the café for a warm cup of coffee.

Cheerful - Noticeably happy and optimistic.

- The man who entered the café on a rainy day was surprisingly cheerful, lifting everyone's spirits.

Aroma - A distinctive, typically pleasant smell.

- The aroma of freshly baked cookies filled Mrs. Parker's kitchen, bringing back fond memories.

Delighted - Feeling or showing great pleasure or satisfaction.

- The townspeople were delighted when Mr. Jenkins offered them free cookies at the bakery.

Satisfied - Pleased or contented because one's expectations are met or exceeded.

- Emily and Jake felt satisfied with how they had managed to brighten people's spirits on a rainy day.

Contentment - A state of happiness and satisfaction.

- Emily felt a sense of contentment as she watched the

rainbow appear after the rain had stopped.

Grateful - Feeling or showing an appreciation of kindness; thankful.

- The townspeople went to bed feeling grateful for the unexpected joy brought by the rainy day.

Connection - A relationship in which a person, thing, or idea is linked or associated with something else.

- The rainy day fostered a sense of connection among the townspeople as they shared stories and enjoyed each other's company.

44.

THE ART
COMPETITION

Emma sat in her small room, staring at a blank canvas. The town's annual art competition was just a week away, and she had yet to start her painting. Emma loved to paint, but this year felt different. The pressure was immense because last year she had won second place. She wanted to do better this time.

Her best friend, Lucas, knocked on her door and walked in. "Hey, Emma. How's it going?" he asked, sitting on the edge of her bed.

Emma sighed. "I haven't started yet. I don't know what to paint."

Lucas smiled. "You always come up with amazing ideas. Remember last year's painting? It was beautiful."

"Thanks, Lucas," Emma replied, smiling slightly. "But I want to do something even better this year. I want to win."

"You will," Lucas said confidently. "Why don't we go for a walk? Maybe it will inspire you."

Emma agreed, and they headed out to the park. It was a sunny day, and the park was full of people. Some kids were playing, and others were having picnics with their families. As they walked, Emma looked around, hoping for inspiration.

"Look at that," Lucas said, pointing to a group of kids playing with colorful kites. "Isn't that beautiful?"

Emma watched the kites soaring high in the sky. They were vibrant and full of life. She smiled. "Yes, it is. Maybe I could paint something with kites."

They continued walking and soon came across an old man sitting on a bench, feeding pigeons. He had a peaceful look on his face. "He looks so content," Emma observed. "Maybe I could paint something that shows peace and happiness."

"That sounds like a great idea," Lucas said. "Just paint what you feel, Emma. That's what makes your art special."

Emma nodded, feeling a bit more inspired. They continued their walk and ended up by the lake. The water was calm, and the reflection of the trees and sky created a beautiful scene. Emma took out her sketchbook and started drawing.

After a while, they headed back home. Emma felt more confident about her painting. She thanked Lucas for the walk and went back to her room, ready to start her work.

For the next few days, Emma spent every free moment painting. She decided to combine all the elements that inspired her during the walk. Her painting featured colorful kites flying in a clear blue sky, an old man feeding pigeons with a peaceful expression, and a serene lake with reflections of trees and clouds.

Finally, the day of the art competition arrived. Emma carefully carried her painting to the town hall, where the event was being held. The hall was filled with beautiful artwork from other young artists in the town. Emma felt a bit nervous but also excited.

Lucas met her there and gave her a reassuring smile. "Your painting is amazing, Emma. I know you'll do great."

The judges walked around, examining each piece of art. Emma watched as they stopped in front of her painting, discussing it quietly. After what felt like an eternity, the judges finished their rounds and it was time to announce the winners.

The head judge stepped up to the microphone. "We have seen some incredible talent today," she began. "It was very difficult to choose, but we have made our decisions. The third place goes to... Sarah Thompson!"

The crowd clapped as Sarah went up to receive her ribbon and prize. "Second place goes to... Michael Brown!"

More applause followed as Michael accepted his award. Emma held her breath, hoping to hear her name next.

"And the first place winner of this year's art competition is... Emma Clark!"

Emma felt a rush of joy and disbelief. She walked up to the stage, her heart pounding. The head judge handed her the blue ribbon and a certificate. "Congratulations, Emma," she said with a warm smile. "Your painting truly captured the beauty of simple moments."

"Thank you so much," Emma replied, her voice shaking with excitement.

After the awards ceremony, Lucas found her and gave her a big hug. "I knew you could do it, Emma! Your painting is incredible."

Emma smiled, feeling proud and happy. "Thank you, Lucas. I couldn't have done it without your help and support."

They walked around the exhibition, admiring the other artworks. Emma felt inspired by the talent and creativity around her. She realized that the competition wasn't just about winning; it was about expressing herself and finding joy in her art.

As they left the town hall, Emma looked at the blue sky, now dotted with kites from the nearby park. She felt a sense of peace and fulfillment. The art competition had brought out the best in her, and she knew that she would continue to paint and find inspiration in the world around her.

Immense - Extremely large or great, especially in scale or degree.

- Emma felt immense pressure to win first place in the art competition after coming in second last year.

Confidently - With a feeling or belief that one can rely on someone or something; in a self-assured manner.

- Lucas reassured Emma confidently that her painting for the competition was amazing.

Vibrant - Full of energy and life; brightly colored.

- Emma's painting featured vibrant kites soaring in a clear blue sky, capturing the essence of movement and color.

Serene - Calm, peaceful, and untroubled; tranquil.

- The serene lake with reflections of trees and clouds inspired Emma to include it in her painting for the competition.

Reassuring - Serving or intended to remove someone's doubts or fears; comforting.

- Lucas gave Emma a reassuring smile before she entered her painting in the art competition.

Exhibition - A public display of works of art or other items of interest, typically held in an art gallery or museum.

- Emma and Lucas walked around the exhibition, admiring the creativity and talent of the other young artists.

Fulfillment - The achievement of something desired,

promised, or predicted.

- Winning first place in the art competition brought Emma a sense of fulfillment and accomplishment.

Expression - The process of making known one's thoughts or feelings, especially in a creative way.

- The art competition wasn't just about winning for Emma; it was about expression and sharing her creativity with others.

Inspiration - The process of being mentally stimulated to do or feel something, especially to do something creative.

- The walk in the park with Lucas provided Emma with inspiration for her award-winning painting.

Joy - A feeling of great pleasure and happiness.

- Emma felt joy and disbelief when she was announced as the first place winner of the art competition.

45.

THE LUCKY PENNY

It was a brisk autumn afternoon when Lily first spotted the glimmer of copper on the sidewalk. Stooping down, she picked up the penny with a grin, turning it over in her fingers. To most people, it was just a coin, easily overlooked amidst the bustle of the city. But to Lily, it felt like a sign—a tiny token of good fortune amidst the mundane.

She slipped the penny into her pocket and continued on her way to the small café where she worked part-time. As she wiped down tables and took orders, her mind kept wandering back to the penny. It wasn't about its monetary value; rather, it was the symbolism behind it. The idea that something so small could hold such significance fascinated her.

That evening, after her shift ended, Lily found herself lost in thought as she walked home. She lived in a cozy apartment on the outskirts of town, where the streets were quieter and the stars shone brighter. As she climbed the steps to her building, she reached into her pocket and felt the penny once more. It was almost as if it had become a talisman, a reminder of the unexpected joys that could come from the simplest of things.

Inside her apartment, Lily placed the penny on her dresser, where it caught the last rays of sunlight filtering through the window. She sat on her bed, gazing at it thoughtfully. Her thoughts drifted to her job at the café, her dreams of becoming a writer, and the uncertainties that lay ahead.

The next morning, Lily woke up with a renewed sense of purpose. She decided to carry the penny with her wherever she went, a silent companion in her journey through life. It became a source of inspiration, reminding her to embrace every opportunity and to believe in the magic of small beginnings.

Weeks turned into months, and Lily noticed subtle changes in her life. She started writing more frequently, jotting down stories and ideas that had been swirling in her mind for years. She submitted a few pieces to local magazines and was pleasantly surprised when one of them got published. It was a small victory, but it meant the world to her.

Emboldened by her success, Lily took a leap of faith and enrolled in a writing workshop. Surrounded by fellow writers, she felt a sense of belonging she had never experienced before. The feedback she received was invaluable, helping her refine her craft and grow as a storyteller.

As she delved deeper into her writing, Lily found herself drawing inspiration from everyday moments—the sound of rain tapping against her window, the laughter of children playing in the park, the aroma of freshly brewed coffee at her favorite café. Each experience added depth to her stories, making them resonate with readers on a deeper level.

One evening, as Lily sat at her desk writing a new story, she glanced at the penny resting beside her laptop. It had become a symbol of her journey—a journey of self-discovery, creativity, and resilience. She realized that finding the penny wasn't just a stroke of luck; it was a catalyst that had set her dreams in motion.

Years later, when Lily looked back on her life, she couldn't help but smile at the memory of that ordinary penny that had brought her extraordinary fortune. It had taught her that sometimes, the most profound changes start with a single moment of serendipity—a found penny on a rainy afternoon.

And as she continued to pursue her passion for writing, Lily carried the lessons of the lucky penny with her, grateful for the courage it had inspired and the opportunities it had unlocked.

Glimmer - A faint or wavering light; a glimpse or hint.

- Lily first spotted the glimmer of copper on the sidewalk, which turned out to be a lucky penny.

Talisman - An object believed to bring good luck or have magical powers.

- The penny became a talisman for Lily, reminding her of the unexpected joys in life.

Renewed - Restored to a better or more vigorous condition; revived.

- Waking up with a renewed sense of purpose, Lily felt ready to pursue her dreams of becoming a writer.

Resilience - The ability to recover quickly from difficulties; toughness.

- The lucky penny symbolized Lily's resilience in pursuing her passion for writing despite challenges.

Serendipity - The occurrence and development of events by chance in a happy or beneficial way.

- Finding the penny on that autumn afternoon was a moment of serendipity that changed Lily's life.

Belonging - Feeling that one fits in or has a rightful place in a particular setting.

- Lily felt a sense of belonging among fellow writers at the workshop, where she received valuable feedback.

Embodied - Represented in physical form; expressed or exemplified.

- The penny embodied Lily's journey of self-discovery and

creative growth as a writer.

Subtle - Not obvious or noticeable; delicate or precise.

- Over months, Lily noticed subtle changes in her life as she pursued her writing more seriously.

Victory - A successful result achieved in a competition, battle, or endeavor.

- Getting her story published was a small victory that encouraged Lily to continue writing.

Embrace - Accept or support willingly and enthusiastically.

- The penny reminded Lily to embrace every opportunity that came her way, no matter how small.

46.

THE BRAVE FIREFIGHTER

Once upon a time, in a quiet neighborhood nestled on the outskirts of a bustling city, there lived a firefighter named Jake. Jake was known for his courage and quick thinking in emergencies. He had joined the fire department right after finishing his training, driven by a deep desire to help others in times of peril.

One chilly autumn evening, as the sun dipped below the horizon, Jake received an urgent call on his radio. There was a fire raging in a residential area not far from his station. Without hesitation, Jake and his team jumped into their fire engine and sped toward the scene.

When they arrived, they were greeted by a chaotic scene. Thick plumes of smoke billowed from a two-story house, and panicked neighbors gathered on the sidewalks, watching in fear. Jake could hear the distant sound of sirens as more fire trucks rushed to join them.

"Stay back, everyone! We've got this under control," Jake shouted reassuringly, though he knew the situation was dire. Flames licked at the windows, casting an eerie glow against the night sky. Inside the house, a family of four was trapped, unaware of the danger closing in around them.

Jake wasted no time. He and his team swiftly donned their protective gear and charged into the burning building. The heat was intense, and smoke stung their eyes, but they pressed on, guided by their training and determination to save lives.

Through the haze, they found the staircase leading to the second floor. With precision and care, Jake led the way, calling out to the family, urging them to follow his voice. "This way! Stay low and cover your mouths!"

Coughing and frightened, the family emerged from a bedroom, clutching each other tightly. Jake's heart raced as he guided them toward safety. "Keep moving! You're almost there," he encouraged, his voice steady despite the chaos around them.

Just as they reached the stairs, a loud crash echoed through the house. Part of the ceiling collapsed, sending sparks and debris tumbling down. Without hesitation, Jake shielded the family with his own body, ensuring they were unharmed.

Finally, they burst through the front door, gasping for fresh air as the cool night embraced them. Jake and his team led the family to safety, where they were quickly checked by waiting paramedics. Tears of relief streamed down the mother's face as she thanked Jake profusely for saving her children.

"It's all in a day's work," Jake replied modestly, though inside, he felt a swell of pride. His bravery had made a difference tonight, ensuring that a family would live to see another day.

As the firefighters worked tirelessly to extinguish the blaze, Jake reflected on the events of the evening. Being a firefighter wasn't just a job to him; it was a calling. Every day brought new challenges and risks, but moments like these made it all worthwhile.

By the time the sun rose, the fire was finally subdued. The neighborhood slowly returned to normal, grateful for the firefighters who had risked their lives to protect them. Among them stood Jake, tired but content, knowing that he had made a difference in the lives of those he had sworn to serve.

And so, the story of the brave firefighter spread throughout the neighborhood, a testament to courage, selflessness, and the unwavering dedication of those who answer the call to serve others.

Peril - Serious and immediate danger.

- Jake joined the fire department driven by a deep desire to help others in times of peril.

Chaotic - In a state of complete confusion and disorder.

- When Jake and his team arrived at the scene, they were greeted by a chaotic scene with thick smoke and panicked neighbors.

Eerie - Strange and frightening.

- Flames cast an eerie glow against the night sky as Jake approached the burning house.

Dire - Extremely serious or urgent.

- Jake shouted reassuringly to the neighbors that they had the situation under control, though he knew it was dire.

Swiftly - Quickly and promptly.

- Jake and his team swiftly donned their protective gear before charging into the burning building.

Precision - The quality of being exact and accurate.

- With precision and care, Jake led the way up the staircase to rescue the trapped family.

Coughing - Making a harsh noise with one's breath due to irritation of the throat or lungs.

- The family emerged from the bedroom, coughing and frightened from the smoke.

Unharmed - Not injured or damaged.

- Jake shielded the family with his body during the collapse, ensuring they were unharmed.

Profusely - To a great degree; in large amounts.

- The mother thanked Jake profusely, tears streaming down her face, for saving her children from the fire.

Subdued - Brought under control, typically by force.

- By the time the sun rose, the firefighters had finally subdued the fire that had threatened the neighborhood.

47.

THE DANCING SHOES

In a quaint town nestled amidst rolling hills and lush greenery, there lived a girl named Lily who had always harbored a deep passion for dancing. From a young age, she would sway and twirl to the rhythm of any music that caught her ear, her feet tapping out melodies only she could hear.

Lily's fascination with dance blossomed during the town's annual festival, where performers from far and wide would gather to showcase their talents. She would watch with wide-eyed wonder as dancers spun gracefully on stage, their movements weaving tales of joy and sorrow, love and longing.

"I wish I could dance like that," Lily would often whisper to herself, her gaze fixed on the dancers' enchanting routines.

But Lily's dreams seemed out of reach. Her family, though loving and supportive, struggled to make ends meet. Her father worked long hours at the local bakery, while her mother cared for her younger siblings at home. There was little time and even fewer resources to spare for extracurricular activities like dance lessons.

Despite the odds, Lily's determination remained unshaken. She would spend hours practicing in the quiet corners of their small house, imagining herself performing on stage with effortless grace. Her bedroom became a sanctuary where she could lose herself in the music and let her body express the emotions she held within.

One fateful day, while exploring the town's bustling market, Lily stumbled upon a curious shop tucked away between a bakery and an old bookstore. Its sign, weathered and faded, read "Magical Finds". Intrigued, Lily pushed open the creaky door and stepped inside, the faint jingle of a bell announcing her arrival.

The shop was filled with an assortment of oddities—glowing crystals, ancient books, and peculiar trinkets that seemed to whisper secrets of times long past. At the back of the shop, on a velvet cushion displayed under a glass dome, sat a pair of shoes unlike any Lily had ever seen.

They were delicate ballet shoes, shimmering with an otherworldly glow that seemed to dance with the light filtering through the shop's dusty windows. Lily's heart fluttered as she approached them, drawn inexplicably to their beauty.

"Ah, those are the Dancing Shoes," a voice crooned from behind the counter, startling Lily. She turned to see an elderly woman with kind eyes and a knowing smile. "They say those shoes possess a magic that can make dreams come true."

Lily's eyes widened with wonder. Could these shoes be the key to fulfilling her deepest desire? Without hesitation, she mustered the courage to ask the elderly woman about them.

"They belonged to a talented dancer long ago," the woman explained, her voice tinged with nostalgia. "Legend has it that whoever wears these shoes will be blessed with the ability to dance like no other, but at a price only the heart understands."

Lily hesitated for only a moment before making a decision. With a determined nod, she asked the woman how much the shoes cost, willing to sacrifice anything to make her dream a reality. The woman smiled knowingly and replied, "For you, child, they are free. The shoes have chosen you."

Overwhelmed with gratitude, Lily slipped the Dancing Shoes onto her feet, feeling an immediate warmth spread through her body. It was as if the shoes had been waiting for her all along, their magic embracing her with a promise of endless possibilities.

That night, Lily danced under the stars in a secluded clearing near the edge of town. The music of the forest accompanied her every move, echoing the rhythm of her heart. With each pirouette and leap, she felt a newfound sense of freedom and joy, her worries and fears melting away.

Word of Lily's extraordinary talent spread like wildfire through the town. Soon, she was invited to perform at local events and gatherings, captivating audiences with her grace and passion. The once shy and reserved girl had blossomed into a confident and radiant dancer, her dreams finally taking flight on wings of magic.

But as the days turned into weeks and the weeks into months, Lily began to notice a subtle change within herself. The magic of the Dancing Shoes was undeniably powerful, but it came with a price she hadn't anticipated.

Her days were now consumed with dance, leaving little time for anything else. She missed family gatherings and outings with friends, her focus solely on perfecting her craft. The shoes demanded her dedication, pushing her to the limits of physical and emotional exhaustion.

One evening, after a particularly grueling practice session, Lily found herself staring at her reflection in the mirror, her eyes tired and her spirit weary. She realized with a pang of sadness that the magic of the Dancing Shoes had come at the cost of her connection to the world beyond dance.

Faced with a difficult decision, Lily returned to the Magical Finds shop, her heart heavy with uncertainty. The elderly woman greeted her with a knowing smile, her eyes twinkling with understanding.

"You have discovered the true nature of the shoes," the woman said gently, as if reading Lily's thoughts. "Their magic is powerful, but it is not meant to overshadow the other joys in your life."

With a heavy heart, Lily removed the Dancing Shoes and placed them on the counter. The warmth she had felt earlier faded, leaving a void she knew would take time to heal. But as she turned to leave, a sense of peace washed over her, knowing she had made the right choice.

From that day forward, Lily continued to dance, not with the aid of magic, but with a renewed sense of purpose and balance. She joined a local dance troupe, where she found friendship and camaraderie among fellow dancers who shared her passion.

Her performances were no longer fueled by enchantment, but by sheer determination and love for the art form. Each step she took reminded her of the journey she had undertaken, the lessons she had learned, and the strength she had discovered within herself.

As for the Dancing Shoes, they remained in the Magical Finds shop, waiting patiently for another dreamer whose heart resonated with their magic. And though Lily had returned to a simpler life, she carried with her the memories of dancing under the stars, guided by the light of a pair of shoes that had once changed her life forever.

Harbor - To keep or hold in the mind.

- Lily had always harbored a deep passion for dancing since she was a young girl.

Fascination - A strong attraction or interest.

- Lily watched the dancers with wide-eyed wonder,

fascinated by their graceful movements.

Sanctuary - A place of refuge or safety.

- Lily's bedroom became a sanctuary where she could practice dancing undisturbed.

Intrigued - Aroused curiosity or interest.

- Lily was intrigued by the curious shop filled with magical items.

Enchanting - Delightfully charming or attractive.

- Lily whispered to herself, mesmerized by the dancers' enchanting routines.

Nostalgia - A sentimental longing or affection for the past.

- The elderly woman spoke with nostalgia about the dancer who once owned the magical shoes.

Sacrifice - To give up something valued for the sake of other considerations.

- Lily was willing to sacrifice anything to fulfill her dream of becoming a dancer.

Radiant - Bright with joy, hope, or health.

- Lily blossomed into a confident and radiant dancer after wearing the magical shoes.

Exhaustion - A state of extreme physical or mental fatigue.

- Lily felt exhaustion creeping in after days consumed with dance practice.

Camaraderie - Mutual trust and friendship among people who spend a lot of time together.

- Lily found camaraderie among fellow dancers in the local dance troupe.

48.

THE HELPFUL GHOST

In a quaint old house at the edge of a sleepy village, there lived a family named the Thompsons. The house, with its creaky floors and vintage charm, had been in the family for generations. It was said to be haunted, though not by a malevolent spirit, but by a friendly ghost named Emily.

Emily had been a young girl when she passed away many years ago, and she had chosen to stay in the house she loved so dearly, watching over its inhabitants with a gentle and caring spirit. The Thompson family, unaware of Emily's presence, often attributed odd occurrences—like misplaced keys or mysteriously opened windows—to mere coincidences.

One rainy autumn evening, as the wind howled outside and raindrops pattered against the windowpanes, the Thompsons found themselves facing a series of unfortunate events. Mr. Thompson had lost his job unexpectedly, leaving the family in a financial bind. Mrs. Thompson, a teacher at the local school, worried about making ends meet while caring for their two young children, Lily and Thomas.

"It's going to be alright, dear," Mrs. Thompson reassured her husband, though her own worries weighed heavily on her mind. "We'll figure something out."

Meanwhile, upstairs in the attic, Emily watched the family with concern. She had grown fond of the Thompsons over the years, admiring their resilience and love for each other. Determined to help in any way she could, Emily decided it was time to make her presence known.

That night, while the family slept soundly in their beds, Emily gently nudged Lily awake with a soft whisper. "Psst! Lily, wake up," she urged, her voice barely more than a whisper carried on the wind.

Lily blinked sleepily, wondering if she had dreamt the voice. But then she heard it again, clearer this time. "Who's there?" she whispered back, glancing around her darkened room.

"It's me, Emily," the ghost replied, appearing before Lily as a shimmering figure bathed in moonlight. "I want to help your family. Will you help me?"

Lily's eyes widened in surprise, but she felt a warmth and kindness emanating from the ghostly presence. "How can I help?" she asked eagerly, curious to see what Emily had in mind.

Emily explained her plan quietly, her words echoing with determination and hope. Together, they would find a way to ease the Thompsons' burdens and bring a smile back to their faces.

The next morning, Lily approached her parents with newfound confidence, excitement bubbling inside her. "Mom, Dad, I have an idea," she began, her voice tinged with anticipation. She told them about Emily and her offer to help, recounting the ghost's gentle presence and desire to support them in their time of need.

Mr. and Mrs. Thompson exchanged a surprised glance, unsure of what to make of Lily's story. But seeing the earnestness in her eyes, they decided to trust their daughter's intuition.

"We have nothing to lose," Mrs. Thompson remarked with a small smile. "Let's hear what Emily has in mind."

That evening, as the family gathered in the cozy living room, Emily appeared once more, her ethereal form glowing softly in the lamplight. She shared her plan with the Thompsons —a series of small, seemingly coincidental events that would bring unexpected blessings into their lives.

First, Emily guided Lily to an old trunk in the attic, hidden beneath layers of forgotten memories. Inside, they found a collection of antique jewelry—precious heirlooms passed down through generations. With Emily's help, they were able to sell the jewelry at a local antique shop, fetching a sum of money that provided temporary relief from their financial worries.

Next, Emily orchestrated a chance encounter between Mr. Thompson and an old friend who happened to be looking for someone with his exact skills and experience. The job offer came at just the right moment, offering stability and hope for the future.

As weeks turned into months, Emily continued to work her magic, leaving small notes of encouragement and guidance for the family to find. She helped Mrs. Thompson discover a forgotten recipe book in the kitchen, filled with delicious recipes that she could share with her students as part of a cooking class fundraiser.

Through it all, Emily remained a silent guardian, watching over the Thompsons with unwavering devotion. Her presence brought a sense of comfort and reassurance to the family, reminding them that they were never truly alone in their struggles.

One evening, as autumn gave way to winter and snowflakes danced outside the window, the Thompsons gathered around the fireplace, reflecting on the events of the past months. Lily and Thomas giggled as they recounted their adventures with Emily, their faces glowing with joy and gratitude.

"We owe so much to Emily," Mr. Thompson remarked, his voice filled with emotion. "She's been our guardian angel."

"And she always will be," Mrs. Thompson added softly, her eyes sparkling with tears of happiness. "We may not see her, but we can feel her presence in every moment of our lives."

As the years passed, the Thompsons never forgot the kindness and generosity of their helpful ghost, Emily. Her legacy lived on in the stories they shared with friends and neighbors, a testament to the power of friendship, hope, and the unseen magic that binds us together.

And though Emily's time with the Thompsons eventually faded into memory, her spirit continued to watch over the old house at the edge of the sleepy village, ready to lend a helping hand to those in need.

Quaint - Attractively unusual or old-fashioned.

- In the quaint old house, the Thompsons lived a peaceful and contented life.

Malevolent - Having or showing a wish to do evil to others.

- The ghost was not malevolent; instead, Emily was known for her kind and helpful nature.

Resilience - The capacity to recover quickly from difficulties; toughness.

- The Thompson family's resilience was evident in how they faced and overcame their financial challenges.

Ethereal - Extremely delicate and light in a way that seems too perfect for this world.

- Emily appeared as an ethereal figure, glowing softly in the moonlight.

Earnestness - Sincere and intense conviction; seriousness.

- Lily spoke with earnestness about Emily's desire to help

their family.

Orchestrate - To arrange or direct the elements of a situation to produce a desired effect, especially surreptitiously.

- Emily orchestrated a series of events that brought unexpected blessings to the Thompson family.

Guardian - A defender, protector, or keeper.

- Emily became a silent guardian for the Thompsons, watching over them during difficult times.

Legacy - Something handed down from an ancestor or predecessor.

- Emily's legacy of kindness and generosity remained in the hearts of the Thompson family.

Unwavering - Firm and determined; resolute.

- Emily's unwavering devotion to the Thompsons never faltered, even in challenging times.

Lend a hand - To offer help or assistance.

- Emily was always ready to lend a hand to the Thompsons when they needed it most.

49.

THE MOUNTAIN CLIMB

In the heart of the Rocky Mountains, where jagged peaks kissed the sky and pine trees whispered secrets to the wind, a group of adventurous souls gathered at the base of Mount Evercrest. Among them were Sarah, a spirited young woman with a love for nature, and her friends Max, an experienced climber with a knack for navigating treacherous terrain, and Lisa, a photographer whose keen eye captured the beauty of the world around her.

They had come together with a shared goal: to conquer the summit of Mount Evercrest, a towering behemoth that challenged even the most seasoned climbers. The mountain loomed before them, its snow-capped peak glistening in the early morning sun, a testament to nature's raw power and beauty.

"We can do this," Sarah exclaimed with determination, her voice echoing off the rocky walls that surrounded them. "Together, we'll reach the top!"

Max nodded in agreement, his eyes scanning the route ahead with a mix of excitement and respect for the mountain's formidable presence. "It won't be easy," he cautioned, "but with careful planning and teamwork, we can overcome any obstacle."

And so, their journey began. With backpacks loaded with supplies and hearts filled with anticipation, the group set off along the winding trail that led to the base camp. The air was crisp and invigorating, the scent of pine needles mingling with the faint hint of adventure that hung in the air.

As they hiked, they encountered fellow climbers from different corners of the world—each with their own stories of triumph and perseverance. There was Miguel, a jovial mountaineer from Spain with a penchant for storytelling, and Mei Lin, a quiet but determined climber from China who moved with grace and precision.

Together, they formed an unlikely alliance, united by their shared passion for exploration and the thrill of testing their limits on the unforgiving slopes of Mount Evercrest.

The journey to base camp was arduous but exhilarating. They crossed icy streams, navigated narrow ridges, and scaled rocky cliffs with the agility of mountain goats. Along the way, they shared meals cooked over a crackling campfire, swapping tales of past adventures and dreams for the future.

As they approached base camp, nestled in a sheltered valley beneath the watchful gaze of the mountain, they were greeted by the warmth of a roaring fire and the camaraderie of fellow climbers who had already made it this far. Tents dotted the landscape like colorful mushrooms, a temporary village bustling with activity and the promise of rest before the final ascent.

The next morning dawned bright and clear, a perfect day for their summit bid. The group gathered at the base of the mountain, adjusting their gear and mentally preparing for the challenges that lay ahead. Sarah's heart pounded with a mix of excitement and nervous anticipation, her gaze fixed on the distant peak that seemed to touch the sky.

"We've come this far together," Max said, his voice steady and reassuring. "Let's take it one step at a time, supporting each other along the way."

With a silent nod of agreement, they set off, their footsteps synchronized in rhythm with the mountain's heartbeat. The trail grew steeper, the air thinner, but their determination remained unwavering. They relied on ropes and harnesses to navigate sheer cliffs and ice-covered ledges, their movements calculated and precise.

At times, doubt crept into their minds as fatigue gnawed at their resolve. But they drew strength from each other—Sarah's unwavering optimism, Max's steady leadership, Lisa's creative perspective captured through her camera lens, Miguel's infectious laughter, and Mei Lin's quiet determination.

Together, they pushed through moments of uncertainty, celebrating small victories—a tricky pitch conquered, a breathtaking vista unveiled, a shared meal under a star-studded sky. Friendship blossomed amidst the challenges, forging bonds that transcended language and cultural barriers.

As they neared the summit, the air grew thin and their bodies weary, but their spirits soared with the knowledge that they were on the verge of achieving their goal. The final stretch tested their endurance and resilience, each step bringing them closer to the pinnacle of Mount Evercrest.

And then, after hours of grueling effort and unyielding determination, they stood triumphant at the summit, their hearts overflowing with a sense of accomplishment and awe. The world lay spread out beneath them like a patchwork quilt, a testament to the beauty and vastness of the natural world.

"We did it," Sarah exclaimed breathlessly, her eyes shining with tears of joy and exhaustion. "We made it to the top!"

Cheers erupted from the group as they embraced each other, their exhilaration mingling with a deep sense of gratitude for the journey they had shared. They stood in silence for a moment, absorbing the breathtaking panorama around them —the sweeping valleys, towering peaks, and endless horizon stretching to the distant horizon.

As they began their descent, their spirits buoyed by the memories they had created and the friendships that had blossomed along the way, Sarah glanced back at Mount Evercrest with a mixture of reverence and fondness. It had tested their limits and challenged their resolve, but it had also brought them together in ways they had never imagined.

And as they returned to the base camp, greeted by applause and congratulatory hugs from fellow climbers, they knew that their adventure on Mount Evercrest had not only been a physical journey but a journey of the heart—a testament to the power of teamwork, determination, and the unbreakable bond of friendship forged amidst the towering peaks of the Rocky Mountains.

Treacherous - Very dangerous and difficult to deal with.

- Max was known for his skill in navigating treacherous terrain during mountain climbs.

Formidable - Inspiring fear or respect through being impressively large, powerful, intense, or capable.

- Mount Evercrest was a formidable challenge for even the most experienced climbers.

Invigorating - Making one feel strong, healthy, and full of energy.

- The crisp mountain air was invigorating as they began their hike towards the summit.

Camaraderie - Mutual trust and friendship among people who spend a lot of time together.

- The climbers shared a sense of camaraderie as they gathered around the campfire.

Exhilarating - Making one feel very happy, animated, or elated; thrilling.

- The view from the summit was exhilarating, with breathtaking vistas in every direction.

Unwavering - Steady or resolute; not wavering.

- Sarah's unwavering determination helped the group stay focused during the challenging climb.

Synchronized - Happening at the same time and speed; coordinated.

- The climbers moved with synchronized steps as they approached the final ascent.

Triumphant - Having achieved victory or success; victorious.

- The climbers felt triumphant as they reached the summit of Mount Evercrest.

Resilience - The capacity to recover quickly from difficulties; toughness.

- Lisa showed resilience in continuing to capture stunning photos despite the challenging conditions.

Reverence - Deep respect for someone or something.

- Sarah looked back at Mount Evercrest with reverence, reflecting on the journey they had undertaken.

50.

THE LOST KEY

On a crisp autumn morning in the bustling city of Rivertown, where cobblestone streets wound through narrow alleys lined with quaint shops and cozy cafes, a young woman named Emma found herself in a most peculiar predicament. It all began when she stumbled upon a weathered key nestled between the pages of an old book at the local antique bookstore.

The key was unlike any Emma had ever seen—its intricate design hinted at a forgotten past, its surface adorned with delicate patterns that shimmered in the soft light filtering through the dusty windows of the bookstore. Curiosity piqued, Emma carefully plucked the key from its resting place, a sense of adventure stirring within her.

"Excuse me," Emma called to the elderly shopkeeper who was meticulously arranging a display of vintage photographs. "Do you know anything about this key?"

The shopkeeper glanced up, his eyes twinkling with a hint of mischief. "Ah, that key has quite the tale to tell," he replied cryptically, his voice tinged with intrigue. "It is said to unlock a door that leads to unexpected places."

Intrigued by the shopkeeper's words, Emma thanked him and left the bookstore, the key clutched tightly in her hand. She couldn't shake the feeling that her discovery was more than mere coincidence—that it held the promise of an adventure waiting to unfold.

Later that afternoon, Emma found herself standing before a

weathered door tucked away in a quiet corner of Rivertown, the key trembling slightly in her hand. The door, adorned with peeling paint and a rusted handle, seemed out of place amidst the bustling cityscape that surrounded it.

With a deep breath, Emma inserted the key into the lock and turned it slowly. There was a faint click, followed by the creaking of hinges as the door swung open, revealing a narrow staircase descending into darkness. Heart racing with a mix of excitement and apprehension, Emma took the first tentative step into the unknown.

The staircase led to a dimly lit underground passage, its walls lined with ancient stone and flickering torches casting eerie shadows. Emma's footsteps echoed softly as she ventured deeper into the labyrinth, guided by the faint glow of the key clasped tightly in her palm.

As she navigated the winding corridors, Emma's senses were assailed by the musty scent of age-old secrets and the faint murmur of voices carried on the whispering breeze. She could almost feel the weight of history pressing down upon her, the passage of time etched into every stone and crevice.

Suddenly, Emma stumbled upon a hidden chamber bathed in soft golden light, its walls adorned with intricate tapestries depicting scenes of forgotten legends and mythical creatures. In the center of the chamber stood a pedestal, upon which rested a gleaming artifact—a jeweled crown that sparkled with the brilliance of a thousand stars.

Mesmerized by the sight before her, Emma approached the pedestal with reverence, her fingers trembling as she reached out to touch the ancient artifact. But before she could grasp it, a voice echoed through the chamber—a voice as old as time yet filled with a youthful vigor.

"Stop right there," the voice commanded, startling Emma. She turned to see an elderly man with wise eyes and a gentle smile emerge from the shadows. He wore robes adorned with symbols of a forgotten era, his presence commanding respect and curiosity.

"I am the Guardian of this chamber," the man explained, his voice a soothing melody that resonated with ancient wisdom. "You have unlocked the door to a realm of secrets and treasures long lost to the sands of time."

Emma listened intently as the Guardian recounted the history of the artifact—a crown once worn by a benevolent ruler who had protected the kingdom from darkness centuries ago. The crown held immense power, capable of bringing prosperity and harmony to those who wielded it with a pure heart.

"But with great power comes great responsibility," the Guardian cautioned, his eyes searching Emma's soul. "Only one who is worthy can claim the crown and fulfill its destiny."

Moved by the Guardian's words, Emma hesitated. She had embarked on this journey seeking adventure, but now she found herself faced with a choice that would shape the course of history. Should she take the crown and embrace its power, or leave it behind to preserve the delicate balance of the world?

After a moment of contemplation, Emma made her decision. With a solemn nod, she stepped away from the pedestal, leaving the crown undisturbed. "I am not the one destined to wield this power," she said softly, her voice tinged with both regret and relief.

The Guardian smiled knowingly, a sense of pride and respect shining in his eyes. "You have shown great wisdom and humility," he praised, his voice echoing through the chamber. "Your courage has unlocked more than just a door—it has unlocked the path to self-discovery and understanding."

As Emma made her way back through the underground passage, the key safely tucked into her pocket, she reflected on the lessons she had learned. Sometimes, the greatest adventures were not about seeking treasure or power, but about discovering the strength and courage within oneself.

When Emma emerged into the daylight once more, the bustling streets of Rivertown greeted her with familiarity and warmth. She returned the key to its rightful place at the antique bookstore, a smile playing on her lips as she bid farewell to the shopkeeper who had started it all.

And though her adventure had come to an end, Emma knew that the memories and lessons she had gained would stay with her forever—a reminder of the day she unlocked a door and found far more than she had ever imagined.

Predicament - A difficult, unpleasant, or embarrassing situation.

- Emma found herself in a peculiar predicament when she discovered the mysterious key.

Intricate - Very complicated or detailed.

- The key had an intricate design that hinted at a forgotten past.

Curiosity - A strong desire to know or learn something.

- Emma's curiosity was piqued by the shopkeeper's mysterious story about the key.

Intrigued - Aroused the curiosity or interest of; fascinated.

- Intrigued by the shopkeeper's words, Emma decided to explore further.

Adventure - An unusual and exciting, typically hazardous, experience or activity.

- Emma felt a sense of adventure stirring within her as she

held the key.

Antique - Belonging to an earlier period, style, or fashion; old and often valuable.

- The key was found in an old book at the local antique bookstore.

Unshakeable - Unable to be changed, weakened, or destroyed.

- Emma couldn't shake the feeling that her discovery held the promise of an adventure.

Apprehension - Anxiety or fear that something bad or unpleasant will happen.

- Emma's heart raced with a mix of excitement and apprehension as she opened the door.

Labyrinth - A complicated irregular network of passages or paths in which it is difficult to find one's way; a maze.

- Emma ventured deeper into the labyrinth, guided by the faint glow of the key.

Reverence - Deep respect for someone or something.

- Emma approached the pedestal with reverence, her fingers trembling as she reached out to touch the artifact.

Made in the USA
Middletown, DE
22 November 2024

65190541R00176